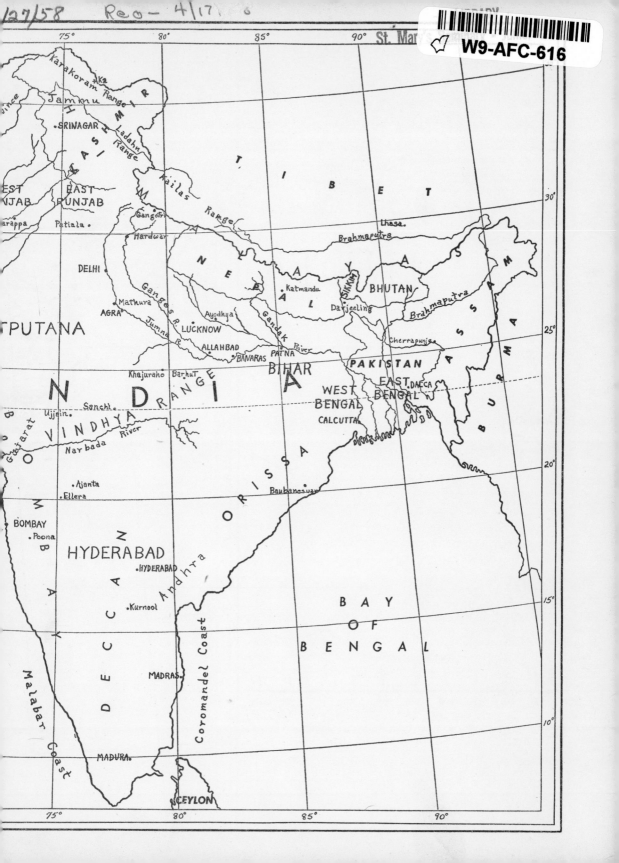

India Today!

India Today!

by

Jack Finegan

 The Bethany Press
St. Louis, Missouri

8588

Preface

The purpose of this book is to give a concise, objective account of India as it is today. This new nation in an ancient land is of such strategic significance in Asia, as Asia is in the world, that it is desirable to learn as much as possible about it. A beginning is made with fundamental facts of geography and ethnography, then the largest city is described where one sees a concentrated cross section of Indian life. The almost bewildering diversity of Indian life is next analyzed so that some of its amazing, as well as appalling, aspects stand out clearly. Back of the complex picture of the present lies an extremely long history, and when this is surveyed, the origin of many elements in the modern scene appears. Naturally the work of archeology is important in the study of Indian antiquity. Following the history into the present we see how the work of Gandhi, Nehru, and others led to the achievement of Indian independence and the establishment of the sovereign democratic republic which is the present state. The results of the first general election in 1951-1952 allow us to chart the relative positions of the many different political forces in India and to evaluate the position of Communism most recently made even more evident in events in newly formed Andhra. India's problems are enormous, especially in the fields of population, economics, and social life, but in addition to assessing the difficulties, it is now possible to describe actual attacks upon them particularly as being made under the present Five Year Plan. In international affairs there is no doubt of India's importance, but the nature of her alignments and purposes deserves attention and indeed requires study in order to be comprehended. Interestingly enough, international notice often is focused upon India not only for political reasons but also for reasons of sport and high adventure. It is impossible to omit mention of the world's highest mountains which are on the northern frontier of the Indo-Pakistani subcontinent, and of the almost incredible epics of courage which have been written in the endeavors of climbers from many nations to ascend their summits. So many religions have such deep roots in India that any attempt to understand how people there think and act must take full account of these faiths. Accordingly, both the religions which originated in India and those which were introduced from the outside are discussed, and the endeavor is made to see their relationships to what is at present going on in Indian life. One of the religions which was brought to India from afar was Christianity. This faith, which now has a long history behind it in India and occupies an important place there, will undoubtedly be an influential factor in what happens in the future life of the nation. Yet the currents of recent happenings are such as to raise many questions with regard to the status of the Christian movement in India and to pose many problems for the Christian church in that land and for those who are related to it as fellow members of the world-wide Christian community. Therefore the final chapter is devoted to an account of the introduction and development of Christianity in India and an assessment, in as honest terms as possible, of its present situation and future outlook.

It is hoped that this book has the accuracy which comes from careful research and also something of the concreteness and vividness which are inseparable from personal experience. My residence and travel in India were in 1952 and 1953, and I record my appreciation for a Fulbright award for research in India in archeology and religion which made this possible.

8

Much of the book was in fact written in India and is based upon what I learned there by observation, conversation, and contact with many different individuals and groups, and close attention to current events as recorded in the Indian press. The author acknowledges with thanks permission from *The Statesman*, Calcutta, to make the quotations on pages 37, 38, 107, 108, 127, 148, 149; and from *The Christian Century*, for quotations on pages 150, 174, 193, 194. Acknowledgment for illustrations is made in the Index of Photographs.

JACK FINEGAN

Pacific School of Religion
University Christian Church
Berkeley, California

Contents

11

Introduction

The author of this readable account of contemporary life and thought in India has succeeded to an extraordinary measure in accomplishing a task usually not easy for a foreigner. Obviously, years of careful study of the historical background, in preparation for the visit to the country where most of the actual writing was done, are responsible for the rare insight and sympathetic understanding which are apparent in almost everything with which he deals in this book. As a keen student of archeology and the history of religions, Dr. Finegan realizes that any worth-while study of contemporary conditions in India needs to be done both in the historic perspective of the past and the revolutionary context of the present.

Dr. Finegan's main concern is to interpret India as it is today to the modern American reader. The book is therefore more than a mere traveler's record. It is not a diary of random observations accumulated in the course of a rapid tour of the country. It is the result of close study and careful observation made possible during months of settled residence in Calcutta and of unhurried travel to other parts of India over a period of nearly two years. During this

13

time he had the unusual advantage of living in friendly and intimate relation with different groups of people, people of all sorts, in India. This experience has enabled Dr. Finegan to get something of an inside view of the land and its people, with its varied contrasts of colour and shade. This myriad view can be somewhat bewildering to any foreign visitor, until he has learned to see beyond what strikes the eye to catch the dim outlines of a new framework of society which is still in the making.

A faithful picture of India today will have to show the strange mix-up of the old feudal order of life, by no means extinct, and the new industrial pattern of society, not yet totally accepted. Dr. Finegan's profile of the city of Calcutta is thus in the main truthfully drawn, though it might strike the cursory reader as inconsistent, and perhaps a bit self-contradictory. But that is India today, for it is currently involved in the hazardous task of evolving a reintegration of culture, in which fragments of the old traditional pattern and bits of the new "imported" forms of life are being pieced together to form a new scheme.

Dr. Finegan has attempted to draw pointed attention to matters of special significance to the American public, because it is needful that they be intelligently informed about the new forces that make the old lands of Asia pulse with new vigour. At the same time they should be made aware of the tortuous problems confronted by Asian peoples which adjustment to the new-world conditions involves. One of the most helpful sections in this book is the survey of contemporary problems in India, and it is based on scholarly investigation of data, secured from many sources, which are as authoritative as they are revealing. Dr. Finegan's concern is primarily to create lively interest in contemporary world affairs, for he writes with no ulterior motive, no preconceived theory or any desire for propaganda.

This would particularly apply to the last section of the book which deals with the many religious groups and communities found among the people of the country. Undoubtedly religious differences contribute no little to the diversity of Indian life and tend to create difficult problems for the national government. And Nationalism, in turn, has given rise to a recrudescence of Hinduism, the religion of

14

the majority. In a country which is striving to realize the ideal of a secular democracy, the tendency to Hinduize Indian culture and the unwillingness of the majority religious group of Hindus to recognize the rights of other minority religious groups can make things difficult. Dr. Finegan's impartial survey of this aspect of Indian life has brought out the present significance of persisting differences in the living religions, and the need to reckon with the principle of religious liberty, which alone can secure the future of India in the world tomorrow. Christianity, in some ways new to India and in other ways as old as the history of Christianity itself, is given a rightful place in this book, as also another "indigenous" religion, and not merely a foreign missionary outpost.

> PAUL DAVID DEVANANDAN, PH.D., *Secretary*
> *Department of Literature and Publications*
> *Council of Y. M. C. A.'s of India, Pakistan,*
> *and Ceylon*

Bangalore, India

1 Portrait

of Land and People

The geographical area which has long been known as India is now the home of two nations, India and Pakistan. Speaking of the entire region from the standpoint of geography, it may be called the Indo-Pakistani subcontinent. It is a land mass of great size which projects southward as a peninsula from the mainland of Asia, yet is plainly separated from the rest of Asia by the mighty wall of the Himalayas. Still considering this subcontinent as a whole, it is approximately 2,000 miles from north to south in its greatest length, and 2,000 miles from east to west in its greatest breadth. Tapering sharply as it does in triangular form to the south, the total area is some 1,500,000 square miles. Thus defined, if a map of the subcontinent is placed on that of North America with the northern limit at the boundary line of the United States and Canada, the southern tip of India is at Mexico City; and with the eastern border between India and Burma placed not far from the eastern seaboard of the United States, the western frontier of Baluchistan extends westward of Salt Lake City. But if the super-imposition of maps is carried out with due regard for respective latitudes and the upper limit of the Indo-Pakistani subcontinent is kept at

37 degrees north, or about at Norfolk, Virginia, then the lower tip at 8 degrees north reaches down into Colombia, South America.

In the division of the subcontinent between the nations of Pakistan and India, Pakistan received areas in both the northwest and the northeast. These were Baluchistan, Sind, the Northwest Frontier Province, West Punjab, and East Bengal. Still in dispute between Pakistan and India are Jammu and Kashmir, a beautiful and mountain-girt region in the extreme north. Existing as independent kingdoms, yet of necessity closely related to India by reason of their geographical position, are Nepal, Sikkim, and Bhutan, all pressed closely up against the Himalayan rampart in the north. Excluding these areas which now constitute Pakistan or are otherwise separate political entities, India itself occupies a territory of some 1,200,000 square miles.

Three great regions are readily distinguishable within the subcontinent. The first is the mountain wall in the north. The main range is that of the Himalaya, "the abode of snow." This is a mountain system 1,600 miles in length, with many peaks over 25,000 feet in elevation. Among them, Mount Everest at 29,141 feet is the highest known summit on earth. To the west and north of the Himalayas is the Karakoram or "black mountain" range, itself several hundred miles in length, with the peak K2, 28,250 feet in altitude, the second highest in the world. These tremendous mountains provide a barrier on the north of India which throughout past history has been all but impenetrable. There is a caravan route which comes through from Lhasa to Kalimpong and Darjeeling in West Bengal; and another which comes out of Tibet to Leh in Ladakh and then descends to Srinagar in Kashmir. In times past only the plodding feet of hardy men and beasts of burden have been able to negotiate these passes of great height. In the extreme northeast on the Burmese frontier the hills are lower and the passes easier, but the jungles are so dense that this has scarcely been an open route. It is in the northwest on the frontier of Afghanistan that the most used land routes into the subcontinent are found. Here the mountains are lower and there are many passes including the famous Khyber. It is this route that the historic invaders of India have taken, from the Aryans to Alexander to the Muslims.

18

The northern mountains not only provide a natural boundary for India but are a source of wealth as well. Their lower slopes are heavily covered with forest and teem with animal life. Terraced fields on steep hillsides provide extensive tea plantations. How rich the mineral deposits may be can scarcely yet be estimated. From the melting snows of the high peaks come the waters for the great rivers which provide for the fertility of all north India. Jawaharlal Nehru says, "I see in the Himalayas the greatest reservoir of power in the world."

The second geographic region is that of the great river plains. Three major streams are fed by Himalayan snows. The Indus has its source in the glaciers of the Kailas Range on the northern side of the Himalayas. From there it flows northwestward, pours through defiles in the Ladakh Range, continues along the foot of the Karakoram, and finally bends southwestward to run down across the Punjab and Sind and empty into the Arabian Sea. Starting at an elevation of over 15,000 feet, it has a course of over 1,500 miles, and its basin is estimated at 370,000 square miles. In Sanskrit this great stream was called *sindhu*, meaning river; in Persian this was *hindu*, and the river valley was Hinduka; and from that the Greeks made the words *Indos* for the river and *India* for the land. Thus the Indus River not only watered the northwest but also gave its name to the entire land. Five important tributaries also flow into the Indus, the Jhelum, Chenab, Ravi, Beas, and Sutlej, and the region they traverse is called the *Punjab* meaning the "five waters."

The ultimate source of the Ganges is at a glacier near Gangotri, over 10,000 feet high in the Himalayas. At Allahabad it is joined by the Jumna which rises farther west in the Himalayas; at Patna the Gandak flows in from Nepal. The last two or three hundred miles of its 1,500 mile course is through a broad delta where it flows through many mouths into the Bay of Bengal. The westernmost of these channels is the Hooghly, on which, ninety miles from the bay, is Calcutta. Between Calcutta and the bay the fall of the river is only an inch or two in a mile; so flat is the entire valley that nearly a thousand miles from its mouth the river is only 500 feet above sea level.

The Brahmaputra rises north of the Himalayas like the Indus and at a place not too far from the source of the latter, but it flows east rather than west and finally turns south and breaks through the mountains only toward their eastern end. Originating at a point over 15,000 feet high and flowing for hundreds of miles at an altitude of 12,000 feet, it plunges down through such precipitous gorges that it emerges on the southern side of the range at only 1,000 feet elevation. In Tibet it is known by various names, and the epithet *Tsangpo*, meaning "the purifier," is given to it as to other large Tibetan streams. In India its proper name is Brahmaputra, which means "son of Brahma." Rolling down across Assam and Bengal it joins the Ganges and, 1,800 miles from its source, pours into the Bay of Bengal.

The plains through which these rivers flow are the richest and most fertile part of the entire subcontinent. The snow-fed waters of the great streams are a dependable source for irrigation. The soil produces abundantly, and rice, wheat, sugar cane, jute, and many other crops flourish. The river valleys were the home of the earliest civilizations in the land, and today about two-thirds of the population of India live here.

Geographically, the third region of the Indo-Pakistani subcontinent is the triangular southern part of the land, most of which is a plateau. It is called the Deccan, from the Sanskrit word *dakshina* meaning "the south." The northern rampart of the area is established by the Vindhya mountains which, with subsidiary ranges, stretch for over 800 miles from west to east and rise to heights of from 1,500 to over 4,000 feet. Like sentinels on either flank of this barrier stand Mount Abu in the west and Parasnath Mountain in the east, 5,650 and 4,482 feet high, respectively. On the southern side of the Vindhyas flows the Narbada River, often taken as marking the boundary proper of the Deccan. Other mountain ranges run down along the sides of the peninsula and are known as the Western and Eastern Ghats. The plateau thus enclosed averages from 1,000 to 3,000 feet in elevation, while there are hills and peaks rising to as much as 7,000 and 8,000 feet. At the foot of the Ghats are strips of fertile coastland, among which the district of Malabar in the extreme southwest is specially famed. The hill country of the Deccan is rich in iron, manganese, gold, mica, and lime, while cotton, millet, rice, pepper, and coffee are grown on the western coast, and sugar cane, tobacco, spices, coconuts, and cinchona on the eastern.

In a country which extends from well above the Tropic of Cancer to within eight degrees of the equator, and from high mountains to low valleys and coasts, it is evident that great ranges of climate will be found. In general, however, the determining factor is that of the two monsoons. These are seasonal winds which sweep across all south Asia, the southwest monsoon from the middle of April to the middle of October, the northeast monsoon from the middle of October to the middle of April. The southwest monsoon reaches the Indo-Pakistani subcontinent after crossing vast stretches of ocean, and is heavy-laden with moisture; it brings 90 per cent of the rainfall which the land receives. The northeast monsoon blows across extended land areas and is accordingly dry. The actual climate resultant from the latitude, the monsoon patterns, and other factors, is marked in much of the land by three seasons. Taking Calcutta for a specific example, the relatively cool weather extends from mid-October to mid-February. December and January are the coldest months, the average low temperature at this time being 56 degrees. The hot season is from mid-February to mid-June. During this period the temperatures climb steadily. In April and May the average high is 95 degrees with individual readings, of course, often being much more. Then the clouds pile up mountain-high in the sky as the monsoon sweeps up the Bay of Bengal. The rains begin and continue for months with intervals of a few hours or a few days. Temperature readings are still in the eighties or nineties and the humidity is usually higher than the temperature, figures of 98 and 99 per cent relative humidity being frequently recorded. By the end of a year 75 or 100 inches of rainfall may be registered. Yet such are the extremes in the entire land that at Cherrapunji in Assam the annual average is around 500 inches, while in desert regions of Rajasthan in the west it may be only an inch or two.

22

The land which has just been described is inhabited by a complex and polyglot population. Fundamentally this population appears to have arisen by a process of intermixture among dark-skinned Dravidians who lived there at an early time, light-skinned Caucasians and other invaders who came in later over the passes in the northwest, and yellow-skinned Mongolians who entered in the northeast from China and Tibet. Since the Dravidians are now found largely in the south it would appear that they were partially pushed ahead of as well as partially amalgamated with the successive waves of incomers in the northwest and northeast.

The result of this process of displacement and amalgamation is the existence of the six main physical types which are commonly recognized. The Dravidians are the first of these. They are a short people and very dark in complexion, somewhat resembling the tribes of Sumatra and Malaya. Having presumably been forced southward by invaders, they are found now from the edge of the Ganges region to the lower tip of the peninsula and also in Ceylon. The Indo-Aryans are tall and fair, with long head, dark eyes, and narrow nose. They are in Kashmir, the Punjab, and Rajasthan, as is understandable if they were indeed once invaders who pressed through the northwestern passes to enter the land. The Aryo-Dravidians are shorter in stature than the Indo-Aryans and somewhat darker; the head is of medium length and the nose medium to broad. They are presumed to have arisen as a mixture of the invading Aryans and the indigenous Dravidians. Known also as the Hindustani type, they occupy the great Ganges valley. The Scytho-Dravidians are of medium stature, with long head and relatively short nose. They are considered an amalgam of Scythian invaders with the Dravidian people. Their home is in the western part of the land, east of the Indus and down into the state of Bombay. The Mongoloid type is clearly recognizable, its representatives having short stature, broad head and flat face, dark, yellow-tinged complexion, and oblique eyelids. Found now in Assam and the eastern Himalayan regions, these people must have originated in China and Tibet. The Mongolo-Dravidians are characteristically of medium stature, with broad head and rather dark complexion. They are judged to be a blend of Mongoloid invaders with Dravidian

23

people, with an admixture also of an Indo-Aryan strain. They include the Bengalis, and are found not only in West Bengal but also in Orissa.

The foregoing classification by main physical types only begins to suggest the complexity of the actual groupings within the population. For one thing, in the long course of history there were many other invaders besides the Aryans, Scyths, and Mongolians mentioned in the preceding paragraph. Greeks, Parthians, Kushans, White Huns, Arabs, Turks, Afghans, and others also came and contributed their part to the racial mosaic of the land. Other factors which contributed to the differentiation of society were the diverseness and separateness of the various geographical areas of the vast subcontinent; the divisiveness of the institution of caste, perhaps in origin a system intended to keep racial groups apart; the multiplicity of religions; and the large number of languages. The dividing lines indicated by these factors cross and recross, and the result is a society comprising the most various groups. In the northwest are powerfully built Baluchis, tall tribal Pathans, and enterprising Kashmiris. In the land of the five rivers are sturdy Muslim Punjabis and Hindu Jats. At home first in the Punjab but found now in many other places are the vigorous and versatile Sikhs. Impelled by their commercial enterprise, the Sindhis have moved out widely from their original habitat in the lower Indus valley. In Rajasthan the Rajput clans maintain the traditions of a martial past. The Gujaratis, many devoted to the Jaina doctrine of nonviolence, are found in widespread enterprises. The Parsis, now much westernized, yet still adhering closely to the Zoroastrian faith, constitute a prosperous and self-contained community in Bombay, with scattered representatives in other cities. In the western hills about Poona are the warlike Marathas who once fought strongly against the Mughals and the British. In the vast valley of the Ganges and Jumna, the Hindustanis maintain the traditions of orthodox Hinduism. In the steaming delta land of the Ganges dwell the sensitive, imaginative Bengalis, with Buddhists, Hindus, and Muslims alike among them. On the slopes of the mighty Himalayas are the homes of the militant Gurkhas, once a Rajput clan, and the mountaineering Sherpas, come like many others in this region over

24

the high passes from Tibet. In the southland are the various Dravidian peoples, the Telugus, Tamils, Malayalam, Kanarese, and others, each group speaking its own language. Back in the hills and jungles are aboriginal tribes such as the Santals and Bhils who may be of more ancient ancestry even than the Dravidians, and out on the Andaman Islands are Negritos of distinct physical type.

The variegated picture presented by these groups is made more colorful by the different manners of dress which they have adopted. The most usual garb of Hindu men is the dhoti. This is a long piece of cloth, usually white cotton or some other material, which is wrapped around the waist and between the legs, and may be worn long or short, and with one or both end pieces tucked in or hanging loose. Muslim men usually wear trousers or a piece of heavy cloth tied around the waist and hanging below the knees. Both Hindus and Muslims, however, in some parts of the country wear pajamas, jodhpur breeches, or other forms of trousers. On the upper part of the body a scarf, shirt, jacket, coat, or other garment may be worn. Some wear fully Western costumes or parts of the same. The most characteristic garb of the Hindu women is the sari, six yards or more of cotton or silk so wrapped as to form both the skirt and the upper part of the dress, with one end of the cloth cast over the shoulder or the head. Graceful in sweep and made in many colors, the sari is doubtless one of the world's more beautiful costumes. Flowing skirts, trousers and tunics, and robes are also worn. The trousers and tunics are worn most by Punjabi women. Robes are worn by Muslim women who are also heavily veiled. Some of them wear a robe made continuous with a head covering which provides only a narrow lattice-work in the front through which to see out. Seventy-seven per cent of the people wear no shoes; those who do, use sandals of wood or leather, slippers, shoes with curving pointed toes, or shoes made after the Western pattern. Headdress varies widely and many, of course, including most of the women, go bareheaded. Hindus, Muslims, and others wear turbans, but these are wrapped in different ways among different groups. Specially distinctive is the Sikh turban, wrapped round the topknot of uncut hair which is a mark of the men of this

faith. Caps and hats range from the fez and the wool hat of the Muslims, to the inverted funnel-like hat of the Parsis, the Gujarati and Nepali hats which are like small ornamented boxes, and the white Gandhi cap worn by many present-day Indians. So great is the variety of head coverings that more than seventy shapes of caps, hats, and turbans have been counted in the city of Bombay alone. Women usually wear their hair oiled, combed, and parted in the middle. Hindu ascetics coil their long hair into a crest in imitation of the god Śiva. Others cut their hair short or long; some shave the entire head except for a single strand of long hair. Both women and men may place a small round spot of ground sandalwood paste colored red or yellow upon the forehead as a mark of caste or of beauty. Coloring is also often applied by the women in the part of the hair and round the edges of the feet. Women wear many gold and silver hair ornaments, earrings, nose rings, necklaces, bracelets, rings, anklets, and toe rings, great differences in usage being apparent in different parts of the country and among different classes and groups of people.

26

The variety of speech is also very great. According to one count, 250 languages are spoken in India. These fall into four main groups which, like the racial types, reflect the long history of the land. The Munda languages are spoken by aboriginal tribes in the hills and jungles of central India, such as the Santals. The Dravidian languages are found in peninsular India, and include Telugu, Tamil, Malayalam, Kanarese, and others. The Tibeto-Chinese languages prevail among the hill tribes of the Himalaya. The Indo-Aryan languages are found throughout the entire northern part of the country. They go back ultimately to the language spoken by the Aryan invaders who came in at an early date from the northwest. This language is generally known as Sanskrit, although in the early form in which it was used for the composition of the Vedas it may be called Vedic or Old Indic. Developing through various stages, Sanskrit became the classical language of the land. Alongside it, however, also arose various dialects of the same language which in general were

27

simpler in grammar and easier in pronunciation. An early one of these dialects was Pali, and many others came into existence which are known collectively as Prakrit. Thus the Buddhist canon is most completely preserved in Pali; the oldest scriptures of Jainism are in Prakrit; and most of the rock and pillar inscriptions of Aśoka found in various parts of the country are in one or another of these dialects. It was from the various Prakrit dialects that the several Indo-Aryan languages now spoken in northern India were derived. Of these, some eight are the most important, and for the most part their names suggest the locale where they prevail. They are Punjabi, Sindhi, Gujarati, Marathi (spoken in Bombay and Hyderabad), Bengali, Oriya (spoken in Orissa), Hindi, and Urdu. Hindi is spoken throughout a vast area stretching from the Punjab to the edge of Bengal. Urdu means "the language of the camp," and is a mixed tongue which arose as a combination of Hindi and Persian, the latter being the speech of the Muslim kings who ruled in this region for centuries. Today Urdu is recognized as the national language of Muslim Pakistan, while Hindi has been declared the official language of India although the constitution allows English to be used for official purposes until 1965. Except for Urdu, often written in an Arabic script, all of the Indo-Aryan languages are written in scripts derived from an ancient alphabet of ultimate Semitic descent known as Brahmi. Scripts likewise descended but more changed and less easily recognized as belonging to the same family are also used for the Dravidian languages in the south.

2 Profile

of a City

A description of Calcutta will provide a view of a cross section of life in India. This is the largest city in the land. According to the 1951 census, Greater Calcutta had 4,550,117 inhabitants. In 1953 it was commonly said that one million persons were sleeping on the streets of the city, and there were thousands of homeless refugees encamped in the Howrah and Sealdah railway stations. An official information bureau estimated at that time that the total number of people in the city was approaching eight million. It may be that such a city is not typical of a land where the majority of the population is rural, and it is certainly true that most of the people of India live in small villages rather than in a metropolis such as this. Nevertheless there are typical villages in the immediate environs of this great city, bullock carts from the country rumble constantly through its streets, and peasants from the land, mountaineers from the north, and even aborigines from the jungle mingle naturally in the crowds. Here, therefore, where so many millions of the people of India are concentrated, there is an opportunity to see many aspects of Indian life.

The airport at Calcutta is at a place called Dum Dum. This name is supposed to come from *damdama,* meaning a raised mound, and is well known from the "dumdum" bullets which have long been made at the government ammunition factory in the vicinity. The airfield is busy, with a traffic of 3,600 flights a month. American, British, Dutch, French, and other international lines touch here, while the planes of the now nationalized Indian airlines radiate out to destinations at home and abroad. On the Indian lines the hostesses wear saris, the pilots are likely to be bearded Sikhs in turbans.

On the long drive from the airport into the city one sees mud and reed huts under the palm trees, then the tenements where a dozen people inhabit a single room, then the four- and five-story buildings of the heart of the city, set in the midst of a confusion of left-hand traffic compounded of buses, trams, autos, oxcarts, rickshaws, coolies, and wandering sacred cows. Early in the morning may be seen multitudes of people who have slept the night through on the sidewalks. Pathetic bundles of rags, they are, just now stirring to life again. All during the day the whole business of living is conducted right on the road. The corner pump or the hydrant which spills dirty Ganges water is the place to bathe, wash teeth, drink, wash dishes, fill jugs. A pot of charcoal is a stove, and a leaf may provide a plate, or else there are a brass bowl and pot to contain food and drink. Eating is done with the fingers.

Throughout the day the streets teem with people. Here is an aboriginal woman with nothing but a scrap of rag for clothing; there a finely attired Sikh with a delicately tinted turban exactly matched to a delicately tinted shirt, and a curled beard held in perfect order by a hair net attached to his ears. Next is an elegant Parsi lady with a gracefully draped sari shimmering with gold, and a handsome Punjabi woman in billowing trousers and tunic and bright silk scarf over her long hair. Along come peasant women with heavy silver jewelry, and babies, naked from the waist down, carried nonchalantly astride the hip. There are men in Western dress, and many more in the dhoti. Occasionally there is an all-but-naked holy man, perhaps with a live snake hanging about his neck.

30

The exotic sights of the city are matched by its many smells. The acrid stench of a wall, the pungent aroma of cooking curry, the fragrant perfume of tropical flowers, and the scent of incense assail the nostrils and mingle to produce an unforgettable composite of odors.

And the sounds are many, too. Late at night there is still heard the creak of a bullock cart lumbering on through the darkness, and the sound of a rickshaw coolie's bell as he continues a nocturnal search for a belated customer. With the first lightening of the sky, roosters begin to call, and innumerable crows begin the cawing they will continue throughout the day. Another bullock cart begins to move: the driver and his cattle have slept on the sidewalk for a few hours and are now going on their way. The sound of water is heard splashing on the street: two men are there with a short length of fire hose, attaching it to the nearest hydrant and flushing off that section of street, then moving on to the next. In the courtyard, bundles of twigs are swishing over the gravel: this is how the sweepers clean the ground. As the day begins, all kinds of itinerant vendors pass along the street, each with his distinctive call or signal. One has an enormous flat tray filled with oranges and apples on his head. He calls out the names of the fruit in the native language with a strong melodious voice.

Another has an equally large basket filled with bright-colored flowers.
The key man carries a box of keys on his head and swings a ring of
keys to make a rhythmic jingle. A tattoo on a small drum is the signal
of the monkey man. He leads two monkeys and a goat which he will
make perform for a small fee. The bear man also uses the same
signal, as he leads a shaggy black bear behind him on a rope. If it is
a pipe which sounds something like a bagpipe it is a snake charmer
with king cobras. One man plays a little flute to advertise the flutes
he wishes to sell. Another plays a lively tune on a small one-stringed
violin which is also for sale. Drum music with bass as well as higher
notes is the trademark of the drum salesman. The brass seller uses
two of his brass plates as cymbals to make known his wares. The man
from the race track, the salesman with the long brushes, and the man
with a basket of live turkeys on his head, all have their distinctive
cries. Unmistakable, too, is the terrible lamentation of the profes-
sional beggar as he goes on his back down the street. These are the
sounds which are heard, these and many more, and after a time each
one summons up in the mind of the hearer the picture for which it
stands.

This swarming, malodorous, clamorous city is the largest in India but it is by no means the oldest; indeed, it is relatively young. The temple of Kalighat, from which Calcutta is said to take its name, is supposed to have been built about 350 years ago. By the middle of the seventeenth century a few British traders settled here in the midst of three Indian villages. At the end of the century, to protect their commercial interests, the first Fort William was built and named in honor of William III, king of England. As the capital of the East India Company, the city grew rapidly, then in 1756 was attacked and taken by an Indian ruler. Most of the British fled, but one hundred and forty-six were captured and on the steaming night of June 20 forced into a guardroom of the Fort, twenty-two by fourteen feet in size. In this "black hole," only twenty-three were alive on the next morning. The following year the famous Clive of India reconquered Calcutta, and after that the city was rebuilt and flourished greatly. Its location on the Hooghly River, one of the branches through which the waters of the mighty Ganges empty into the Bay of Bengal, has made it a natural center of trade and commerce. It is also the capital of the province of West Bengal.

The British influence is still marked in Calcutta, even though India is now free of foreign rule. Indeed, British people are probably better liked there and throughout India than they ever were before. One Indian said to me, "Now they are our guests." Many city streets in Calcutta retain English names, such as Queen's Way and Clive Street. The Victoria Memorial, a large structure of white stone looking something like an American state capital building, houses extensive exhibits relating to English rule and rulers, especially Queen Victoria who was proclaimed Empress of India in 1877. And in spite of the strong movement for the use of the Indian languages by the Indian people, English is still widely known and employed.

Calcutta has large hotels, such as the Grand Hotel on Chowringhee Road and the Great Eastern Hotel on Old Court House Street, which offer accommodations and service patterned much after Western standards. Yet they are by no means devoid of the flavor of the

East, for the doorman is a turbaned Sikh with bandolier and shotgun, and every night homeless Indian people, wrapped in their rags, sleep on the sidewalk immediately outside the door. There are also boardinghouses, with high standards of cleanliness, which cater to the needs of Westerners more permanently resident in the city. Here and in personal residential establishments the "bearer," a hired servant attached to an individual or family, is a universal institution, and the proliferation and stratification of service categories—including cooks, doormen, drivers, nursemaids, sweepers, and others—is very great.

Nearly a dozen moving picture theaters in Calcutta show American and English films, while many more show Indian films and not infrequently ones from Italy, Russia, or Japan. Incidentally Indian films are themselves produced in at least six different languages. There are stage productions of plays, magic, and Indian dancing, while concert artists from the West frequently make Calcutta appearances too.

But the pageant of the streets remains for the most part more remarkable than anything shown on stage or screen. Chowringhee Road, the main street of Calcutta, is a perpetual carnival. Sacred cattle and motley hordes of people mingle on the sidewalk. Beggars and vendors utter their cries. Everything is for sale, from a tiger skin to a green myna bird which a boy holds up on his finger for passers-by to see. On adjacent Park Street a girl from Tibet offers a beautiful display of brass and silver work straight out of the Forbidden Land. Women from the country carry on their heads enormous bright-colored baskets which are for sale for a few rupees. On near-by Russell Street every variety of sidewalk enterprise is under way. Cooking, cobbling, fortunetelling, barbering and manicuring take place on the street. The barber shop is simply a place under a tree where the barber squats down facing his similarly positioned customer and administers the shave and haircut.

Special bazar areas provide for concentration of shops. The Stewart Hogg Market on Lindsay Street, usually called the New Market, was opened in 1874 and now contains something like five hundred

shops, all under cover. Almost anything can be purchased here from a pin to a tailored suit, from candy to jewelry, and from fruit to fish. The Barabazar is a very large bazar in the old or north part of Calcutta, and may be arrived at along Harrison Road. Here there is a veritable warren of streets and alleys lined with open-front stalls, selling cloth and brass and food and everything imaginable. The alleys are extremely narrow and filled with all the odors of the East. Masses of people swarm through them, picking their way around wandering cattle and goats, and pressing themselves back into door-ways to make room for passing rickshaws and bullock carts.

Here in the midst of this primitive and teeming confusion one feels in the very heart of India. Yet overhead an airplane proceeds toward a landing, and one remembers that Dum Dum Airport is as much a part of present-day India as is the Barabazar. The cross section of Indian life provided by Calcutta is, therefore, full of contrasts and it is necessary to study these contrasts more system-atically in order to sharpen the focus of our picture of India.

3 Picture

of Contrasts

The contrasts of life in India are amazing and appalling. There are problems of the most colossal sort and achievements in which great pride can be taken. Among items on the dark side of the picture must be listed the following.

Dirt is everywhere. The sacred cattle, which wander freely even in the streets of the cities, deposit their manure on the steps of banks, stores, and theaters. There it lies until scavenger women gather it up, mold it in their hands into cakes for fuel, and plaster these on walls and trees to dry. Western standards of sanitation are virtually unknown. An acrid stench of overpowering intensity arises from almost every fence and gutter. Coughing and spitting fill the air, and the streets are covered with splotches of red which is the expectorated *pan* or betel-nut concoction so universally chewed. During 1952 a city ordinance was under discussion in Calcutta, but not yet passed, which would prohibit spitting on the floors and walls of restaurants. Concerning a first-class railway train compartment an Indian wrote: "The one I got into was filthy and malodorous; plainly it had not been swept or cleaned for a considerable time. The lavatory was in an even worse state of neglect and lacked every sanitary facility." This description applied to a first-class accommodation; there are also second-class, intermediate, and third-class compartments, usually progressively dirtier and more crowded.

Disease is terribly prevalent. It is recommended by the United States Public Health Service that the traveler to India have inoculations and immunizations for cholera, plague, yellow fever, typhus, typhoid, paratyphoid, tetanus, and small pox, a list of diseases which includes some of the worst historic scourges of mankind. Along with these, India knows the ravages of amoebic and bacillary dysentery, malaria, tuberculosis, elephantiasis, and leprosy. In one week in Calcutta there were 832 deaths: sixty-six persons died of tuberculosis, twenty-nine of dysentery, sixteen of malaria, and six of cholera. In one month almost three hundred people died of tuberculosis. During the past five years, one out of every four babies born in Calcutta died within a year of its birth. Last year, out of 50,424 infants under one year of age, 12,255 died of various diseases. Within the decade there was a year when one out of two babies died. In the state of Bihar there are 1,100,000 known victims of leprosy.

That there is a connection between the horrible dirt and the terrible disease can hardly be mistaken. A newspaper report described the conditions prevailing in most Indian towns in the vicinity of Calcutta as follows: "The principal features are: narrow roads which have been cut to pieces by bullock cart and lorry traffic; conservancy and drainage of the most primitive type, the former being based on the long-outmoded system of service latrines; a profusion of tanks and swamps which form ideal breeding grounds for disease-carrying insects; and gloomy dilapidated houses. The term 'house' is a euphemism for most of the mud huts and ramshackle brick structures which serve as residences in these areas. The water supply in many of these towns is scanty; the principal sources of bathing water are tanks, while ordinary open wells, and in a few places, tube wells, are the main sources of drinking water."[1] It may be added that in villages the stagnant pond known as a tank often provides the water for all purposes including washing ticks off of diseased cattle.

[1] *The Statesman* (Calcutta), September 15, 1952.

This description of "Dining at the Ritz" also appeared in a Calcutta newspaper: "There is a little street in central Calcutta to which evening is particularly kind. Minarets from a near-by mosque cut a violet pattern from the grey-green sky, and the little restaurants and tea stalls that line the inadequate pavements are like caves out of fairy tales, so enchanting is the reflection of colored light bulbs upon the intricacies of China mosaic. . . . But even night cannot hide some of the city's darker secrets. Outside the enchanted restaurant a miserable fowl is being slaughtered to satisfy the taste of that prince-like individual within. It is plucked and cleaned right in the drain that passes under the doorstep, in which two miserable dogs are nosing. A boy hurries out from under a sheet of sacking that might be a curtain of brocade or velvet and carries a tray of soiled plates, cups and cooking utensils to a pavement culvert that even the magic of night cannot quite transform into a fountain. He waits whilst a man finishes his bath and a child its ablutions, and then he casually washes up in the same water, using his shirt tail and sleeves as a dishcloth. No sooner does he return these to the kitchen to be heaped with food and served to the waiting customers, than he visits the culvert again with a kettle and draws off sufficient water for several dozen cups of tea. As an afterthought he washes his face and rinses his mouth. Another youth from a sweetmeat shop near by waits to collect some water. This he will mix with the rapidly disappearing milk that his shop is busily transforming into popular sweetmeats."[2]

The destitution of the people is another element on the dark side of the picture. If the Nizam of Hyderabad was the richest man in the world, as he was said to be, with a reported cash fortune of three hundred million dollars and an annual cash income of six million dollars, among the people of the same subcontinent are certainly some of the poorest in the world. Some are poor because they have lost what they once possessed. When the tragedy of division between India and Pakistan took place, hundreds of thousands escaped across the border lines with only what they could carry. A former professor told me of being awakened in the middle of the night to escape

[2]*The Statesman* (Calcutta), September 15, 1952.

slaughter and of fleeing penniless, leaving behind a million dollars (where a professor got a million dollars in the first place he did not explain). A high-caste Hindu woman told of losing all her property except the few pieces of jewelry she was able to hide in her hair. Just before the new passport and visa system was instituted to control travel between Pakistan and India, thousands more of frightened minority people streamed across the lines. We saw multitudes of them living in railway stations and on railway platforms, subsisting on slight doles, scourged by disease, possessing only what they carried. In January, 1953, over 1,700 were reported living, uncared for, and many the victims of malaria, bronchitis, and dysentery, in Howrah Station, Calcutta. But if some are poor on account of losing what they formerly had, far more of the destitute have never known any other lot.

Many lack sufficient apparel. Destitute women sometimes walk on the streets of Calcutta with nothing but a cloth thrown over the shoulder for clothing; many men have nothing but a loin cloth. Although custom as well as poverty is reflected in the figure, it is significant, as already noted, that only 23 per cent of the population of India wear shoes. Many lack food. Out of 11,672 boys and girls in the free primary schools of Calcutta, 7,210 were suffering from malnutrition and the results therefrom in a recent check. Many lack homes. A survey made in Bombay a few years ago showed that 256,000 persons lived in single rooms shared by six to nine people, 15,000 in rooms shared by twenty or more, and 300,000 slept on the streets. In Calcutta it is said that a million persons sleep on the sidewalks every night. If you pass through the streets in the early morning you see so many such persons that you think the estimate may not be exaggerated. Each pitiful pile of rags is someone who has been there through the night, who will stir to life after a time, go to the sidewalk pump and make his ablutions for the day. This is his only home.

As far as statistics on earnings go, the average individual income in India is reported to be about one hundred and fifty rupees or thirty dollars per year. Peasants have an income of twenty or twenty-five rupees, that is four or five dollars, a month. Those who are higher up the scale still have earnings which seem to us pitifully small. A "bearer," a servant in a household or boarding-house, for example, may receive seventy-five rupees or fifteen dollars per month. A man in government employ, which is much sought after, may have a salary of two hundred rupees or forty dollars per month. It is difficult for an outsider to assess the meaning of these figures accurately. Needs may be simpler than in some parts of the world, prices of necessities lower. Nevertheless, the standard of living which can be maintained on such incomes is at best certainly very low.

One more item on the debit side is the division which exists. The land is divided geographically. At the same time that freedom was achieved in 1947, Pakistan and India were separated from each other. Pakistan is a country, predominantly Muslim in population, which consists of two parts. One part is in the west, and you enter it if you arrive at Karachi. The other part is in the east, and you can fly to its chief city, Dacca, in an hour from Calcutta. The remainder of the subcontinent is India. This division makes no economic sense. The jute industry, for example, is a major factor in the economy of the northeastern part of the land. Most of the jute is grown in East Bengal, most of the jute mills are in West Bengal. Now East Bengal has become a part of Pakistan and is entirely cut off from West Bengal. Thus an artificial barrier has been erected in the middle of an area which is a natural economic unit, and the result is harmful to all concerned. This and other examples are regularly cited when the division is discussed, and I found no one in India who did other than deplore what had happened. I also found no one who thought that what had been done could be undone.

The reason for cutting off Pakistan from India was to establish a separate country for the Muslims, but the religious divisions of this subcontinent are far more complex than to be solved by a simple expedient like that. Even after wholesale population shifts, not all the Muslims are in Pakistan nor all the Hindus in India. In 1952

40

the Muslims made up 86 per cent of the population of Pakistan, and 9 per cent of the population of India. In India, moreover, the Jains, the Parsis, the Sikhs, and others also constitute self-contained religious bodies. Each of these groups is separated from the others by distinct traditions, peculiar beliefs, and customs which are apparently unalterable. Hindus, for example, eat no beef, Muslims no pork or ham, and one could not possibly cook for the other.

The divisions here are not only geographical and religious but also social. The Indian caste system must be the most ramified and rigid stratification of society ever established anywhere. There are four main castes—priests, warriors, traders, and workers. Within each main group there is a multitude of subdivisions. Bearers, cooks, gardeners, launderers, and sweepers are all workers, for example, but no one of them would condescend to perform a task more menial than his own proper labor. Each one bosses the one beneath him with the haughty arrogance of inherited right, until at the bottom of the list the poor sweeper has no one to order around except, perhaps, his own wife.

41

Dirt, disease, destitution, and division—these are some of the appalling aspects of life in India. But on the other hand there are many things which are amazing and wonderful. They are things of which India has every reason to be proud. There is the antiquity of the civilization. Speaking at the Bose Institute in Calcutta, Dr. R. C. Majumdar, former Vice-Chancellor of Dacca University, recently pointed to an area of accomplishment in ancient India not yet sufficiently explored. He declared that the rise of a spirit of rational inquiry into the phenomena of nature could be traced in India five hundred years earlier than in Greece. He showed evidences in the Vedic hymns of early Indian speculation about the five primordial elements and the atomic origin of the universe strikingly similar to the theories of Thales and Anaximander and doubtless preceding them in time, and he described the development of scientific methods of observation, inference, and experiment which led to advances in astronomy, medicine, mathematics, and chemistry comparing favorably with those of any other ancient people. Among numerous other achievements in ancient India we may mention the following almost at random: In the sixth century B.C. the Buddha preached a message of universal love and brotherhood. In the third century B.C. a victorious king, Aśoka, voluntarily gave up further conquest by force of arms and devoted himself to the welfare of his subjects. Already in his time Indian seamen were making voyages of sixty days or more; in the first century A.D. the South Indian port of Cranganore was welcoming Arab and Roman merchants; and in the fourth century A.D. under the Guptas, India was a great maritime power. At the beginning of the Christian Era Indians were using numbers from one to nine with zero and with place-value. In the eighth century this system was adopted by the Arabs and it was through them that it was passed on to the West. That is the reason we describe as "Arabic numerals" what is fundamentally an Indian invention. In the fifth century A.D. a wrought-iron pillar was manufactured in India which could not have been produced anywhere else in the world until the nineteenth century. Twenty-three feet high and weighing six tons, it has not rusted in 1,500 years. In the fifth, sixth, and seventh

42

centuries the world's greatest university was to be found at Nalanda where 10,000 students assembled and scholars came together from Asia and parts of Europe.

India is a land not only of antiquity but also of beauty. From fronded palms silhouetted against a tropical sky in the south to the great white height of Kanchenjunga in the north, and from the exotic flowers of the jungle to the serene lakes of the storied vale of Kashmir, the beauty of nature is striking. The beauty of Indian architecture is world famous. We saw the Taj Mahal first by moonlight, and it floated before us like a cloud upon the horizon. By day, too, we were ready to agree that it is the most beautiful building in the world. Throughout all India there are tombs and palaces and temples so picturesquely located, so handsomely constructed, and so elaborately decorated as to be worthy of a long pilgrimage to see. The beauty of craftsmanship even today is remarkable. The machine age has not yet imposed its standardization upon everything and it is to be hoped that it never will. The textiles of Orissa are hand-woven in the most pleasing patterns. The brocades of Banaras shimmer with threads of pure silver and gold; if in need of cleaning they are sent to a jeweler to be polished. The wood carving of Kashmir fills panels with subtly humorous animal forms peering out of dense forest growth. An ivory box from Old Delhi represents in the intricacy of its carving the labor of half a year. And the daily scene upon the street, with the variety of costumes already described, is attractively variegated and picturesque.

The character of the people excites admiration at many points. A British officer published a letter in India a year or two ago which gave a rather pathetically belated expression to his regard for the bravery and courage of the Indian soldiers who used to serve with him and to his affection for them. Under the leadership of Gandhi, thousands of the same Indian people exhibited that even higher form of courage in which they allowed themselves to be ridden down by mounted police, charged with lathis, and fired upon, without offering any kind of violent resistance. The capacity of the peasants for patient labor on inadequate sustenance is prodigious. The dignity in bearing of

the poorest worker, walking erectly down the street with an incredible load balanced on his head, is noticeable. There is a courtesy and gentleness in the demeanor of many which bespeak a great kindness of heart. There is a widely used Hindu greeting which is one of the most pleasant and meaningful salutations in the world. It consists in lifting the hands and folding them together in front of the face or chest. It means, according to the explanation given me by a high-caste Hindu, a recognition of the divinity in the person so saluted. There is also a sense of humor which is often delightful and which has sometimes helped a poor people not to be overawed by the pomp and circumstance which were exhibited before them. One recalls how when Gandhi was in London, wearing his inevitable dhoti, he was asked if he thought that sufficient covering for his audience with the king. He replied that it would be all right since the king would doubtless be wearing enough for both of them! If one adds to the name of Gandhiji, as he is now affectionately called, the names of Tagore and Sadhu Sundar Singh and many others, one remembers properly how many individuals of outstanding greatness have emerged among the Indian people.

India's determination to be free has written one of the inspiring chapters in the history of the twentieth century. The American people and the Indian people will always have this in common, that both were at one time under the burden of domination by an outside power and both achieved independence. The odds against the attempt on India's part appeared overwhelming. Winston Churchill declared, "We mean to hold our own." Gandhi's cry had about it the fervor of our own Declaration of Independence: "Let us breathe the air of freedom. It may choke us, suffocate us, as it did the slaves on their emancipation. But I want the present sham to end." The struggle is still in the so recent past that it is yet impossible to assess it in fully correct perspective. But the revolutionary method of nonviolent resistance was no less remarkable than the outcome. On August 15, 1947, the representative of the King of England solemnly and officially made India free.

Now the effort is being made to direct the same kind of determination toward the improvement of conditions in free India. One of the most graphic portrayals of India after 1947 was published under the title *Halfway to Freedom*. The title embodies the penetrating observation that the achievement of independence represents only the first half of India's total necessary endeavor. There remains the struggle, which will doubtless be longer and harder still, for freedom from poverty and from all the other denials of human rights which have never yet been overcome. By what means this battle will be conducted, whether by methods of reformation and education in which the spirit of Gandhi still lives, or by techniques of violence and terror introduced by agents of Communism, cannot yet be told. It is certain only that the representatives of the old order of bitter oppression and colossal inequality who wish to do nothing or to do as little as possible by way of change, will be subjected to more and more pressure from the masses of the people who are stirring with the same discontent that is felt throughout all Asia.

It is a picture of contrasts, then, that confronts one in India. There is all that we have described and more. There are temples and beggars, pensioned princes and grinding poverty, sacred animals and starving people, caste and a cry for equality, beauty and horror, disease and drama, death and life. It is a picture which, once seen, is unforgettable. If its dark elements are appalling, its bright side is immensely attractive.

45

4 Pageant

of History

The long history of India provides the background against which the almost bewildering picture of the present can be better understood. The story of Indian civilization extends over some five thousand years and for the purposes of a brief sketch may be divided into five periods.

The first period was that of the Indus civilization. Throughout the world the earliest civilizations arose in the favorable environment of great river valleys. This was true in Egypt, Mesopotamia, and China, and it was also the case in India. The Indus River, it will be remembered, rises north of the Himalayas, cuts through passes into Kashmir, and then flows southwestward to empty into the Arabian Sea at the northwestern corner of the Indo-Pakistani subcontinent. It must have been as early as 3000 B.C. that people began settling in towns on this river and on its famous five tributaries. Within a few hundred years some of the settlements became large cities, and if one had visited them around 2500 B.C., one would have been amazed at their modern appearance and conveniences. The two best-known were at places which today are called Mohenjo-daro and Harappa, but it has not yet been possible to discover what their ancient names

were. At both sites, however, archeologists have excavated and have learned a great deal.

These cities were planned before they were built. Mohenjo-daro was laid out directly beside the Indus and covered two hundred and fifty acres. Its streets ran north and south, and east and west, and intersected at right angles. The main street was thirty-three feet wide. The houses were constructed of burnt brick, which was a durable building material of attractive appearance. Open courtyards provided for outdoor life, and the homes enjoyed private wells and bathrooms. The houses also had rubbish chutes and drainage pipes for the disposal of refuse and waste water. The large street drains with which these connected were made of stone, cemented with asphalt, and covered with removable stones or bricks to make cleaning possible. Thus the standards of cleanliness and comfort were surprisingly high.

The people lived upon grains and fruits grown in the fertile valley, fish caught in the river, and meat from domesticated animals. Grains of wheat and barley, seeds of dates and melons, and bones of animals and fish were found in jars which still remained in the ruins of the kitchens. Artisans made good pottery out of clay from the river bank, covered it with red, and painted designs on that with black. They manufactured many different kinds of utensils and implements out of copper and bronze, and made jewelry and ornaments of silver, gold, ivory, and various stones. Statuettes show that the women wore short skirts and had many rings, bracelets, necklaces, nose ornaments, and adornments for their hair. The men wore beards, and one is portrayed with an elaborate shawl over his left shoulder and under his right arm.

It casts some light on the character of the people to see how many toys they had for their children. These included tiny models of objects used in the house, animals with heads pivoted so they would nod up and down, and two-wheeled carts drawn by humped oxen. The people also made a great many seals which could be stamped upon soft clay to leave an impression. These have pictures of many animals such as the humped bull, the elephant, and the rhinoceros, and other figures. There are also inscriptions on the seals but these have not yet been deciphered.

If we ask about the religion of the people we find evidences of animism and the worship of animals, trees, and stones. Many phallic stones were found, and figurines of the mother-goddess type. Especially interesting is a figure on one of the seals. This is a personage with three faces who is seated on a low platform in the cross-legged position of a yogi. He wears a horned headdress, and is surrounded by wild animals. He must be a god who was worshiped by the people.

In some ways one would think that India had deteriorated rather than progressed since this early period. The houses and sanitary facilities of millions of Indians today are not nearly as good as those of the ordinary residents of Mohenjo-daro long ago. In other regards, time seems to have stood still. Women still adorn themselves in much the same way, and the two-wheeled cart drawn by the humped cattle remains the most characteristic form of transportation. But the most significant clues of all discovered in this early time to help us understand India today are the items of religious belief and practice just indicated. Comparing these with what exists today, there is still much animism in the more remote parts of India. Phallic stones are found in temples and village shrines all over the land.

~~fall, ever-encroaching jungle growth, saltpeter in the soil, salt air~~ Mother goddesses are worshiped as the source of fertility in the villages, the wives of Śiva are very important in everyday religion, and the female principle called *śakti* is discussed in philosophy. The god Śiva, moreover, probably the most prominent single deity in India, appears to be essentially the same as the three-faced god on the Indus seal, since even today he is usually represented with three or more faces, is considered the chief of yogis, and called the lord of beasts. Thus features of the remotest antiquity appear plainly in the face of present-day Indian religion.

The Aryan period is the second in the story of India. It may have been about 1500 B.C. when the Aryans appeared. Where they came from is not known, but their language and beliefs show that at least in the distant past they were related to the Aryans who went into Iran, Greece, and Europe. The Aryans who entered India left an extensive literature written in Sanskrit. The oldest part of it is composed of more than one thousand hymns known as Vedas. The word *veda* means knowledge. This word itself shows how the language of these people was related to that of the other Aryans for it has the same root as Greek *oida*, Latin *videre*, German *wissen*, and English *wit* and *wisdom*. Another example where the similarity is even easier to recognize is found in the Sanskrit word *pitr* which is fundamentally the same as Greek *patēr*, Latin *pater*, German *Vater*, and English *father*. The Aryans who entered India worshiped many gods whom they called *devas* or "heavenly ones," using a word which is related to Latin *deus* and English *deity*. Among the gods was the Sky Father, Dyaus pitr, who is clearly the same as Zeus of the Greeks and Jupiter of the Romans.

The Vedas give us a picture of the Aryans as they fought against their enemies in the Indus valley. Calling themselves *aryas*, which means "kinsmen" or "nobles," they designated their foes as *dasas* or "slaves," and described them as "black-skinned," "nonsacrificing," and "malignant." Driving furiously in chariots and shooting powerful bows, the noble invaders vanquished the darker people. Then, as later literature shows, the Aryans moved on eastward and settled in the valley of the Jumna and the Ganges.

49

Some of the Aryan deities, like Vishnu, one of their sun gods, became important in subsequent Indian religion, and the Upanishads, a late part of the Vedic literature, had much influence upon philosophy. In the Upanishads the essential identity of the soul of man and the soul of the world is taught, and the method of meditation is recommended as the way to attain comprehension of that truth and thereby obtain salvation. The doctrine of reincarnation also is implied. According to this doctrine one passes through an endless cycle of births and deaths, and in each new existence occupies a higher or lower place according to one's karma, which is the result of one's former deeds. In this connection there is reference to the different strata in human society, and here we come upon a form of social organization which may have been established by the Aryans and which has endured ever since. This is the system of caste.

The color prejudice of the Aryans was evident in their disparaging reference to the "black-skinned" folk whom they found in the Indus valley. Alongside this they seem to have developed a class consciousness with regard to the different kinds of work which men did. Thus color and employment were the two criteria according to which the strata of society were differentiated. As time went on, the priests were recognized as constituting the highest class. Called Brahmans, they knew how to conduct the rituals and perform the sacrifices upon which the right relationship of man to the gods was believed to depend. Although one would suppose that the king was originally the most important man in the community, in course of time the rulers and warriors came to be regarded as members of the second class in society. These were the Kshatriyas. The third social class comprised the farmers and traders and craftsmen. They were called Vaisyas. Although they stood in this descending order, all three of these groups—Brahmans, Kshatriyas, and Vaisyas—were regarded highly. Because their young men underwent a ceremony of initiation, they were known as the twice-born. The fourth group was much lower in the scale. This group was made up of the menial laborers, who were called Sudras. When the Aryans conquered the earlier inhabitants of the land, they doubtless reduced many of them to virtual slavery and that is perhaps how this fourth and lowest class originated. Even though they intermarried their conquerors, these people were generally those of darker skins and thus were marked out in that way, too, for inferiority. In order to justify the system further, the myth was invented that the Brahmans, Kshatriyas, and Vaisyas were created from the head, hands, and thighs of the supreme Brahman, the soul of the universe, and that the Sudras proceeded from his feet, thus being destined from the beginning for menial tasks. Low as the Sudras were in society, there were others who were lower still. These may have been primitive folk who fled before the invaders, then returned to the fringes of their settlements to do such repulsive work as that of scavengers. They became known as the "fifths," or "out-castes," or "untouchables."

The caste system, which can be explained plausibly as having developed in some such way as this during the Aryan period, has provided the fundamental structure of Indian society. In the course of time it became both more ramified and more rigid. The main castes were divided into numerous subcastes and, according to one reckoning, there are now 2,718 castes in all. Almost the only way to enter a caste is to be born into it, the only way to leave it is to die, and from birth to death one's work, one's marriage, and almost all the other features of one's life are determined by it. Thus what happened in Aryan times helps us to understand some of the chief features of Indian society today.

The third period in the story we are sketching is that of the great Indian kingdoms and empires. It is not until nearly the sixth century B.C. that we can speak of real history in the generally accepted sense of information about kings and dynasties and dates, and even then the records are still scanty. At that time the northern kingdom of Magadha under the Śiśunaga dynasty was the most important of a number of Indian states. After that, much more inclusive realms were established, notably the empire of the Mauryas, whose greatest king was Aśoka, ruling around 250 B.C., and the empire of the Guptas, founded by Chandragupta I, A.D. 320. In between times the land was recurrently invaded and dominated for shorter or longer periods and in smaller or larger areas by the Persians, Alexander the Great, the Bactrian Greeks, the Sakas, the Parthians, the Kushans, the White

51

Huns, and the Rajputs, most of whom if they stayed long became thoroughly Indianized.

More important for our purpose than to trace the political complexities of these times is to notice that between 600 B.C. and A.D. 1000 most of the major present-day religions of India came into existence and developed their character. Hinduism was evidently the result of a gradual mixture of the religious ideas of the earlier inhabitants of the land and of the incoming Aryans. Two main sects, devoted to the worship of Śiva and of Vishnu, respectively, were formed, and six so-called orthodox systems of Hindu philosophy were set forth. Although Hinduism allows for great varieties of belief, in general it holds that every living creature goes through a long cycle of rebirths, that one's condition in the next birth is determined by karma or the results of deeds in former existences,

52

and that nirvana or escape from the cycle is the ultimate goal. Jainism was promulgated in the sixth or fifth century by Vardhamana Mahavira, a man of royal family who sought truth by practicing extreme asceticism. Jainism agrees with Hinduism about rebirth and karma, but is much more extreme in the application of the principle of noninjury or *ahimsa* in relation to all forms of life. Monks of the stricter sect of the religion follow Mahavira's example in wearing no clothing whatsoever. Buddhism was founded at about the same time by Siddhartha Gautama who obtained the title of Buddha or "the enlightened one" as a result of insight which came to him after long meditation on the problem of human suffering. Buddhism likewise accepts, although with modifications, the doctrines of karma, reincarnation, and nirvana, but is distinguished by its teaching of a middle way which lies between the extremes of sensuality on the one hand and self-punishment on the other. It teaches universal loving-kindness, and in its later form makes much of the ideal of the Bodhisattva who could enter nirvana but remains outside of it in order to help other beings. Late Buddhism also uses many images of Buddhas and Bodhisattvas.

In the first century, according to tradition, Christianity was introduced into India. In the seventh and eighth centuries, Zoroastrians fled into India from Persia where they were being persecuted by Muslim Arabs. In India these Persians became known as Parsis. If we add to the groups just discussed the Animists mentioned earlier and the Muslims and Sikhs who will be told about in connection with the next period in Indian history, we have accounted for the major faiths which are active in modern India.

The Muslim period is the fourth in the historical account of India. This epoch began about A.D. 1001 and lasted to 1707. The Muslim invasions were begun by a Turk from Ghazni in Afghanistan named Mahmud, and within two hundred years the famous Slave dynasty of Muslim rulers was founded in Delhi. After a series of other dynasties the powerful Mughal empire was established, whose most famous kings, ruling in the sixteenth and seventeenth centuries, were Akbar, Jahangir, Shah Jahan, and Aurangzib. As followers of the prophet Muhammad, the Muslims believed in one God, Allah, and were strongly opposed to Hindu idolatry and caste. Beginning with the destruction of the famous temple of Śiva at Somnath by Mahmud, they wrought much havoc with the earlier Indian monuments of art and architecture. For their own part, they erected handsome mosques, palaces, forts, and tombs at Delhi, Agra, and other sites, the most beautiful of all being the Taj Mahal, the mausoleum built by Shah Jahan for his favorite wife, Mumtaz Mahal.

The Sikh religion arose at this time out of interaction between Hinduism and Islam. Its chief founder, Nanak, who lived about A.D. 1500, declared boldly, "There is no Hindu and no Muslim."

54

Endeavoring to transcend religious divisions, he taught monotheism and mystical devotion. He was opposed to idolatry and caste, and established a common kitchen where all could eat together regardless of class or creed. Nanak was known as a Guru or "teacher," and was followed by nine other similar leaders. The adherents of the religion were called Sikhs or "learners." In spite of its eclecticism, the faith of the Sikhs proved acceptable to neither Hindus nor Muslims, and the latter in particular became its persecutors. Sikhism responded by taking on a military character, and the eventual result was the establishment in the nineteenth century of a strong Sikh kingdom in the Punjab.

Of all the many invaders of India throughout the centuries, the Muslims were almost the only ones to remain there permanently and yet not to be absorbed into the great amalgam of Indian civilization and Hindu religion. The doctrine of transmigration, the practice of idolatry, and the system of caste were all repellent to them. About A.D. 1030 a Muslim author known as al-Biruni wrote a work on India in which he described all these things critically. Concerning caste, for example, he said: "We Muslims, of course, stand entirely on the other side of the question, considering all men as equal, except in piety; and this is the greatest obstacle which prevents any approach or understanding between Hindus and Muslims." In very much the same vein, Mohammed Ali Jinnah, founder of modern Pakistan, said: "We have no—and I repeat—*no* sympathies with the Hindu. We eat the cow, the Hindu worships it. We admit no religious inequality, the Hindu lives by caste. He will not eat with us. We cannot live together—I tell you, the Muslims are a nation." Thus what happened in the fourth period of Indian history provides the background for the recent division between India and Pakistan.

The British period is the fifth in the history of India. Six years after Columbus discovered America, the first European, the Portuguese Vasco da Gama, arrived at Calicut on the Malabar coast; in the seventeenth century the Dutch, the Danes, the French, and the English arrived; and by the time England was losing its American colonies it was gaining the prize of India. The death of the Emperor Aurangzib, A.D. 1707, may be taken as marking the beginning of the

British period in India, since from that time on the Mughal power declined rapidly and the commercial penetration of the English traders turned increasingly into military conquest. Under Robert Clive the British overcame the formidable French resistance and reduced French holdings in India to little more than the settlement at Pondichéry; at the same time the British East India Company gained in power and wealth. Under Warren Hastings, Cornwallis, and later governors-general, wars were fought and treaties negotiated which established British power as paramount throughout the land. The challenge to this authority in the Indian Mutiny of 1857 was put down with great severity; in 1877 Queen Victoria was made Empress of India. Some two-fifths of the subcontinent remained in the form of princely states which were allowed to retain a measure of sovereignty in return for their cooperation with the British rule; three-fifths constituted British India. The real masters of 250,000,-000 people were the less than 5,000 men of the British bureaucracy.

In 1885 the Indian National Congress met for the first time, and from then on nationalist sentiment and agitation grew steadily. During World War I in which Indian troops fought bravely, the British government promised ". . . the gradual development of self-governing institutions with a view to the progressive realization of responsible government in India as an integral part of the British Empire." But when a British officer ordered his men to fire upon an unarmed mass meeting in Amritsar in 1919 many Indians felt that the old order was not going to change much under the old rulers. During World War II the Indian National Congress launched a Quit-India campaign against British rule which was conducted for the most part non-violently and ultimately with success. Meanwhile the Muslim League, founded in 1906, worked for the freedom of Muslims from Hindu domination as well as from British government. Because the Muslims and Hindus could not agree, the British rulers left behind not one but two free nations, India and Pakistan, when they departed from this subcontinent in 1947.

That the British period provides the immediate background of the present-day situation in India is plain. It is not so clear just how we should evaluate what the British did for India. On the positive side it may be observed that law and order were established and maintained, and that a Civil Service was built up in which many Indians were trained for administration. Over forty thousand miles of railroad were built, giving India the fourth greatest mileage in the world. Eighty-five thousand miles of road were surfaced, more than in any other country of Asia. Postal, telegraph, and telephone services were developed, and I must say that the rapidity and frequency of mail delivery which I have enjoyed in Calcutta far exceeds that to which I am accustomed in the United States. The British built dams and canals which irrigate fifty thousand square miles of land, and conducted programs of agricultural improvement. Work in medical aid and nutrition was sponsored by the government. The English language was brought into widespread use, providing a common medium of communication and education in a country otherwise handicapped by a multiplicity of languages. The Indian National Congress itself was founded originally by a Briton, Allan Octavian Hume, for the purpose of encouraging political discussion among thoughtful Indians. The Indian census, taken at ten-year intervals, was inaugurated in 1871. The preservation of ancient monuments was considered a responsibility, and a director general of archeology was appointed. On the whole the physical appearance of India was probably better under British rule than it is at present; at any rate, most of those who commented to me about shabby streets and buildings remarked that things had deteriorated in the past five years. Nevertheless, in spite of the tangible benefits of British rule to at least some of which most Indians would doubtless testify, there are few of the people, as far as I can ascertain, who are not glad that the British sovereignty is a thing of the past.

On the negative side of the evaluation must be put the undoubted fact that much wealth was drained from India. It has been said that under Clive "frank spoliation" was the policy. Traders reaping enormous profits and officials living in far more luxury and drawing much larger salaries than they could have had in England, were not in India "for their health." Winston Churchill, trying to hold on to what England possessed, said that India is our "daily bread—that's all." So India provided daily food for a foreign power while her own millions starved. Schools were poorly supported and social life deteriorated in many aspects. Machine industry tended to displace the products of individual artisans and craftsmen. As compared with epochs when Indian art, culture, and philosophy were at their height, the India of the British period presented a sorry sight, although the blame was of course not all on the foreign rulers. Nor can I think that the erection of such expensive monuments to the foreign rule as the Victoria Memorial in Calcutta, a large, elaborate building said to have been intended to rival the Taj Mahal, is a contribution to Indian welfare of which to be particularly proud. And when I found a standard British guidebook to India still devoting more than half of its space on Lucknow to details of the military engagements in the Mutiny of 1857 I could not help remembering that Lao Tzu said a victory in battle ought to be celebrated with rites of mourning. The trouble is simply that there is a spirit alive in the world today which says that all men have the right to be free, and in the light of that glorious truth no imposition of foreign rule upon an unwilling people looks good in retrospect. The great leaders who made the new India were moved by that spirit of freedom.

5 Pursuit

of the Past

Much of our knowledge of the remote past in the Indo-Pakistani subcontinent is based upon the work of archeology in the discovery, excavation, and study of ancient monuments, artifacts, inscriptions, and other materials. In so far as the monuments were visible and known, many of them were objects of interest to travelers and pilgrims even long ago. About A.D. 400 a Chinese Buddhist named Fa Hien left China by the western frontier, crossed the fearsome Gobi desert, came over the high Himalayas, descended into the Indus valley, and so reached India. Then he visited sites which were sacred in his faith. He went to Kapilavastu, near where Gautama Buddha was born, and saw the pagodas which marked spots where particular events transpired in the life of the founder of Buddhism. He went to Gaya and saw where Gautama lived in the years just before attaining enlightenment. There were pagodas and monasteries marking these places too, and he was also shown a cave in which Gautama once dwelt. It is to be feared that Fa Hien was as gullible as were some later tourists, be-cause he reports seeing the shadow of Buddha which was still visible upon the wall. Almost 250 years later another Chinese Buddhist pilgrim, Hiuen Tsang, came to India and left a written account of what he saw. He visited the famous Deer Park near Banaras where the Buddha preached his initial sermon on the way of life he had discovered. Hiuen Tsang saw there a large monastery with fifteen hundred priests, many statues of Buddha made of copper and of gold, and a stone stupa built by King Aśoka which was already partly ruined. At Kusinara he went to see the place where Buddha died and found another ruined stupa built by Aśoka, a tall stone pillar, and an old monastery building with a large figure of Buddha reclining as if asleep, which was a portrayal of his death. In the scriptures of Buddhism it is recorded that before the Buddha died he told his disciples that while after his decease they no longer would be able to come and see him in person, they would always be able to visit the four places where he was born, became enlightened, preached the first sermon, and entered into final peace, and at those spots to have a feeling of reverence and remembrance of him. That was what Fa Hien and Hiuen Tsang were doing as they visited Kapilavastu, Gaya, Banaras, and Kusinara, as a host of other pilgrims animated by the Buddhist faith have done since.

Although he was a Buddhist, Hiuen Tsang also wrote about many Hindu monuments which he saw on his travels in India. At Kanauj he visited two temples, one dedicated to the Sun god, the other to the god Śiva. He says that these structures were built of blue stone of great luster, and ornamented with various elegant sculptures. Each temple had 1,000 attendants to sweep and water it, and the sound of drums and songs was heard day and night. At Banaras he found a hundred Hindu temples, and was struck particularly by a copper statue of Śiva which he describes as one hundred feet high, with a grave and majestic appearance as if it were really alive. The believers in Hinduism have always gone assiduously to these and many other sites of their religion, most of which are marked by temples, statues, or other monuments. Seven cities are specially sacred to the Hindus—Banaras, Hardwar, Ujjain, Mathura, Ayodhya, Dwarka, and Conjeeveram—but hundreds and hundreds of other places are also deemed worthy of pilgrimage.

Muslim travelers also were interested in the monuments of India. Around A.D. 1030, Abu Rihan Muhammad of Ghazni, better known as al-Biruni or "the foreigner," wrote an extensive work telling what he had seen during the time he spent in India. Although as a Muslim he did not believe in images himself, he describes many Hindu idols at length. One which he saw was made of bronze and almost life-size; another of wood, the exterior covered with red leather and with two red rubies for eyes. Also he tells about the various sites and rivers to which pilgrimage was made.

When the British entered India they viewed the monuments of the past with appreciation, and it was due to their efforts that the collection, preservation, and study of Indian antiquities were begun in a modern, scientific way. In 1783 Sir William Jones came to Calcutta as a judge of the Supreme Court and, on account of his own personal interest, began to learn Sanskrit. He then conceived the idea of an institution which would promote the study of oriental literature and culture in general, and suggested this to friends. In January, 1784, within four months of his arrival, a meeting was held in Calcutta and a resolution passed to establish a society whose object would be to inquire "into the history and antiquities, arts, sciences and literature of Asia." So was founded the Asiatic Society. In 1796, only forty years after the inception of the British Museum in London, the Asiatic Society decided to start a museum in Calcutta to house the many antiquities it had accumulated; in 1839 the directors of the East India Company made a grant for the salary of the curator and the maintenance of the museum. This provided the nucleus of the Indian Museum which was established by the Indian Museum Act of 1866 and moved into its own building on Chowringhee Road in 1875. Officers of the Asiatic Society also did important research work. In 1837 James Prinsep, secretary of the Society, discovered the key to the Brahmi alphabet in which the earliest Indian inscriptions were written. A few years later the Kharosthi script was deciphered too.

The establishment of an Archaeological Department in India took place in 1862. At that time General Alexander Cunningham, who had come to India with the Royal Engineers and had given much study to the ancient monuments, was appointed Director of Archaeology. He was expected "to make an accurate description of such remains as most deserve notice, with the history of them so far as it

61

is traceable and a record of the traditions that are retained regarding them." At the time it was thought that he could discharge this assignment within a few years and so bring the project to a close. With fuller knowledge of how many monuments there were, how much they stood in need of measures of preservation, and how ramified and complex was the possible research connected with them, it was seen that the work needed to be continued instead of terminated. General Cunningham was therefore, in 1871, made Director General of the Archaeological Survey of India and called upon "to superintend a complete search over the whole country and a systematic record and description of all architectural and other remains that are remarkable alike for their antiquity or their beauty, or their historic interest." Pioneering in character as the work necessarily was, by the time of his retirement in 1885 General Cunningham and his associates had published twenty-three volumes of reports on Indian antiquities. The successor to Sir Alexander Cunningham, Dr. James Burgess, had already been in charge of archeological work in South India, and he continued in the more responsible post until 1889. He was notable particularly for his work on the cave temples of India.

When Lord Curzon became Viceroy of India, he felt that the government should do far more for archeology than had been done previously. He described what existed in India as "the most glorious galaxy of monuments in the world," and declared, "It is, in my judgment, equally our duty to dig and discover, to classify, reproduce and describe, to copy and decipher, and to cherish and conserve." Under Curzon in 1902 John H. Marshall became Director General of Archaeology in India and continued in the position until 1931. Cunningham had already visited Harappa, R. D. Banerji now discovered Mohenjo-daro, and the excavation of both sites was a great achievement of Marshall's administration. Previous to that time no monuments of note had been known which were earlier than the third century B.C. As Marshall put it after the new excavations, "at a single bound, we have taken back our knowledge of Indian civilization some 3,000 years earlier." Other excavations were undertaken at Pushkalavati, Sarnath, Kasia, and Rajagriha, such Buddhist sites

62

being chosen because the writings of Hiuen Tsang had just been translated and gave information about what to expect, and because there was hope, which proved justified, of making relatively spectacular finds which would attract public interest and increase the support of archeological work. Much was done to preserve monuments already known and to make them accessible to visitors. The beautiful museum at Sarnath was also erected. Associated with Sir John Marshall were such men as E. Hultzsch, the epigraphist; Sir Aurel Stein, the explorer of the Northwest; and Jean Philippe Vogel, later of the Kern Institute in Leyden and editor of the important *Annual Bibliography of Indian Archaeology*. With a view to the future, Marshall instituted a program of training Indian students in archeology; one of the first of these was Ghulam Yazdani.

Archeological work was also done by the Indian states under the princely rulers. In Hyderabad, the Archaeological Department of the state was inaugurated in 1914, and large undertakings were launched to provide access to the notable monuments at Ajanta and Ellora and to preserve them from ruin. A sumptuous photographic publication was also made of Ajanta, with explanatory text by G. Yazdani.

How wise was the expectation that Indians themselves should more and more take over the work of archeology in India is shown by the course of events. From 1937 to 1944 an Indian, Rao Bahadur K. N. Dikshit, was Director General. Following him the post was held by Dr. R. E. Mortimer Wheeler. Then came national independence and the subsequent reorganization which integrated the Department of Archaeology under the Ministry of Education in the Government of India. In 1949 the National Museum of Art, Archaeology, and Anthropology was opened at New Delhi, with present quarters in the front State Rooms of Government House. In 1950 the Department of Archaeology published a book entitled *Archaeology in India* as a summary of what had been done from the earliest beginnings up until that date. In 1953 the Director General of Archaeology in India was Pandit Madho Sarup Vats, M.A., Hony. F.R.A.S., with office in New Delhi.

It is not surprising that much effort has been required simply for the preservation of known and existing monuments. Excessive rainfall, ever-encroaching jungle growth, saltpeter in the soil, salt air by the coast, drifting sand, shifting rivers, and earthquakes are among the natural hazards to which the monuments are exposed. In some cases the depredations of man have been worse than the effects of nature. Muslim conquerors destroyed many temples and sculptures in their iconoclastic zeal. Warfare wrought devastation. Builders carried off material ready-made for their purpose; railroad contractors quarried bricks from the ruins of Harappa. Present-day settlers often inhabit ancient ruins with destructive results; tourists commit acts of vandalism. Famous monuments were in regrettable condition until modern works were undertaken on their behalf. At the Taj Mahal the approaches had to be cleared of squalid bazars, the ruined colonnades of the forecourt rebuilt, and the lawns laid out and trees planted, both of which now give so fine a setting to this noble structure. At Delhi the Mughal gardens in the Fort of Shah Jahan were half destroyed and buried deep under debris; ten years' work was required before the watercourses, fountains, and flowered causeways were again in good condition. At Konarak the Black Pagoda was largely buried under fallen stones and drifted sand. At Ellora the porch of the rock-hewn Kailasanatha temple was crumbling and a steel frame had to be hidden within it to prevent its complete collapse. At Ajanta large sums were required to simply make the famous caves once more accessible. The road leading in that direction from Aurangabad extended for thirty miles, then there were thirty miles of cart track often lost amid boulders and ravines. Now a good highway leads all the way. Nor can the work of preservation ever be neglected without unfortunate results. In 1939 there were 2,662 monuments under the protection of the central government and of these 1,000 were under a program of annual repair. In 1936 roof leaks were discovered in the Taj Mahal; by 1952 over $700,000 had been spent on restoration of pillars and walls spoiled by rainwater; and the planned repair work was continued in 1954. In early 1953 the colossal 57-foot statue of the Jaina saint, Gommateśvara, at Śravana Belgola in South India was coated with a water-repellent substance as a protective measure against the weather and with particular view to the Jaina festival held in March which is celebrated once in twelve years.

64

As for the discovery of hitherto unknown archeological sites and the excavation of ruins not yet touched by the spade, the possibilities must be virtually limitless. Indeed, in the present state of knowledge of the Indian past there are whole areas which are still almost blank. There is, for example, an almost complete gap between the Harappa civilization of 2500-1500 B.C. and the early historical period of around 300 B.C., and there are serious enough gaps between the second century B.C. and the fourth century A.D. New light at these and other points will be most welcome and may be forthcoming at any time, for archeology is a science in which surprising and unexpected discoveries are constantly being made. As a matter of fact, excavations begun in 1952 and carried further in early 1953 at Amreli in Saurashtra were credited in the first press reports with discoveries partly bridging the gap between the post-Harappa and the pre-Mauryan periods.

In what follows, representative examples will be given of archeological museums and monuments in India. Among museums, the three whose establishment has already been referred to earlier in this chapter are specially significant. The National Museum at New Delhi is at present handsomely housed in the marble halls of Government House, and contains some of the choicest exhibits from all over India. Materials from Mohenjo-daro and Harappa are prominent in the collection, for this museum has the finest pieces of art from the Indus Valley civilization. There are statues in stone and metal, beautiful painted pottery, and many examples of the famous Indus Valley seals. The Indian Museum on Chowringhee Road in Calcutta contains geological, zoological, and economic galleries as well as archeological. Standing in the main entrance hall are two huge archaic statues. One is a female figure, shown with plaited hair and elaborate jewelry; the other, which is a cast of an original in the Mathura Museum, is a male figure, with heavy earrings, necklet, and waistband. These are known as a *yakshi* and a *yaksha*, and were probably deities of water and fertility. The statues are believed to date from the second century B.C. Thus from the Indus Valley period we have here come far down to relatively early historical times. In a hall to the right are exhibits of which the Indian Museum is particularly proud. These are the sculptures from Barhut. Barhut is

65

a site in central India where the followers of Buddha built a memorial monument in about the middle of the second century B.C. The main monument, which was in the form of a mound known as a stupa, has been destroyed but the railings and gateways with which it was surrounded were partly preserved and were brought to the museum in Calcutta for safekeeping and exhibition. The pillars and rails are all elaborately carved with statues and bas-reliefs. The main pictures are scenes from the stories known as Jatakas which tell about the many previous existences of the Buddha. The belief is that before he was born as the historical Gautama who became the Enlightened One, the Buddha went through many different lives, being born sometimes as a man, sometimes as an elephant, deer, or monkey, and sometimes even as a tree. These carvings, therefore, show all kinds of events in which animals as well as human beings take part. One scene shows "the holy tree that perfectly gladdens the heart of the deer,'" as the accompanying inscription states. We see a sacred tree with an empty throne below it, the throne being a symbol of the presence of the Buddha who

was not at that time represented in human form. Gathered round
the tree and throne are two lions and six deer, all of which are calmly
standing, sitting, or lying down. Under the influence of the gentleness of the Buddha, the fierce lions have lost their thirst for blood,
and the timid deer have forgotten their fear. Some of the scenes are
enlightened with a delightful humor. In one case a man's tooth is
being extracted by an elephant pulling an enormous forceps with a
cable under the supervision of a group of monkeys; in another, monkeys set at the task of watering plants are carefully pulling up the
plants to see how large their roots are so they will know how much
water to pour on! The Indian Museum also has a rich collection of
medieval Hindu sculptures from Bengal, Bihar, Orissa, and other
parts of India.

Compared to the two very large institutions just mentioned, the Sarnath Museum is relatively small; nevertheless it is most attractive. It displays the antiquities found at this place, a few miles north of Banaras, where the Buddha preached his first sermon. Appropriately enough, the building itself is constructed on the plan of an ancient Buddhist monastery except that instead of small cells there are large halls for the exhibits. The first object to be seen in the main hall is the handsome capital of the column which was erected in the third century B.C. by King Aśoka to mark this famous site. The base of the capital is bell shaped, then there is a drum ornamented with carvings of a lion, an elephant, a bull, a horse, and wheels, and seated above back to back are four magnificent lions which once supported a stone wheel of the law. Another object is a world-famous statue of the Buddha. Made of white sandstone, it shows the Buddha seated upon a throne, with a beautiful nimbus behind his head and disciples at his feet. Dating from the Gupta period, this statue is probably

68

one of the finest ever made to portray the founder of Buddhism. Many other images, reliefs, terra cottas, and architectural fragments are in the same museum.

Above, mention was made of the now-destroyed Buddhist stupa at Barhut. The finest example of a stupa that is still reasonably intact is to be seen at Sanchi, between Bhopal and Bhilsa in Central India. Although Sanchi is now a remote and normally quiet place, it was once teeming with life. Not far away was Vidisa, one of the capitals of ancient India, and at Sanchi itself were large monasteries. King Aśoka put up a pillar here, with an inscription, and his queen is said to have had a residence at the place. It is also narrated that their son, Mahendra, paid a visit to this vicinity before setting out on his famous mission to preach Buddhism in Ceylon. The Great Stupa at Sanchi is supposed to have been built first as a structure of brick by Aśoka in the third century B.C., to have been greatly enlarged in the next century, and to have been ornamented with the handsome gateways which are its particular pride in the first century B.C. As seen at Sanchi, a

stupa is fundamentally a hemispherical dome surrounded by a processional path and enclosed by balustrades and gateways. In its earliest origins a stupa was doubtless just a burial mound. Then it was used by Aśoka and others as a monument to enshrine a relic of the Buddha or of his disciples. As such it was visited by pilgrims who came as an act of piety to circumambulate the holy remains. The gateways of the Great Stupa at Sanchi are covered with sculptured scenes from the life of the Buddha and from his previous existences. Like the sculptures at Barhut, those at the Great Stupa of Sanchi belong to the early time when the Buddha was represented only by symbols, although when it was an event in one of his previous lives, if he was then a man, he is shown in such form. Among the symbols used are the lotus which stands for the birth of the Buddha, the tree which represents his enlightenment, the wheel which suggests his first sermon, and the stupa which connotes his death. In portraying the great renunciation there is shown only a horse with an umbrella, the sign of royalty, held above the empty saddle, and this represents Gautama riding away from his home. Interestingly enough, the horse is carved four times in succession to show the progress of the trip, then at the end is pictured once more turning back to the city after Gautama has gone away on foot. Such were the "moving pictures" upon which the ancient pilgrims gazed and which are still to be seen at Sanchi.

World famous are the Buddhist caves at Ajanta. The site is a secluded valley sixty miles north of Aurangabad in the state of Hyderabad. The Waghora River flows through this valley and plunges down in a series of waterfalls. The ravine curves in a picturesque crescent and the walls rise in steep rock cliffs. Here, in a period extending from before the Christian Era to the seventh century A.D., twenty-nine caves were excavated and decorated with carvings and paintings. The finest artistic work was done in the fifth and sixth centuries at the height of the Gupta period. Many of the caves were used as viharas or monasteries. Cave Number One is a splendid example. A columned veranda gives access to a central hall about 65 feet square, the roof of which is supported by twenty columns. On the sides are the cells in which the monks dwelt, and at the back is a shrine within which looms up a colossal statue of the Buddha. The entire interior of the cave was once covered with paintings, and enough of these remain to give a good idea of the color and beauty which then existed here. Since Buddhism teaches compassion for all things, the paintings comprise a veritable pageant of animal and human life in ancient Indian times. There are princes and princesses, snake charmers and soldiers, elephants and monkeys. Upon the back wall is a superb figure of a Bodhisattva who gazes upon the whole variegated scene with tenderness and sympathy. Some of the caves were chaityas, that is Buddhist chapels, and of these Cave Number Twenty-six is a good example. Nearly seventy feet in length and over thirty-five feet wide and thirty feet high, the hall has side aisles formed by a colonnade of twenty-six pillars. The arching roof is decorated with stone ribs which suggest that this excavation in stone is patterned after chaitya halls built of wood. Above the entrance a large horseshoe window permits light to fall upon the stupa which stands at the apsidal end of the sanctuary. The stupa is covered with representations of the Buddha, all round the hall are other reliefs, and at one side is a colossal reclining image which portrays the entry of the Buddha into nirvana at death. Some of the caves and some of the sculptures were begun but not finished, and part of the interest of Ajanta lies in the opportunity it offers of studying all stages of the process by which these remarkable works were accomplished.

Ellora is in the same region as Ajanta, perhaps forty miles away, and there it is possible to see rock-hewn caves and temples, twelve of which were excavated by the Buddhists, seventeen by the Brahmans, and five by the Jains. Cave Number Twenty-nine, one of the Hindu group, has a striking location. Entering its great hall, you proceed to a recess on the south side and look out upon the curving wall of the ravine at the very point where, in the rainy season, a waterfall plunges over the cliff and falls into a small lake below. The central hall itself is about 150 feet long and 100 feet wide. The roof is carried by heavy pillars, and the general appearance is much like that of the Elephanta cave temple at Bombay. Indeed the two caves belong to the same period of about the seventh century A.D. There are many sculptures of Śiva and other Hindu deities on the walls of the

Ellora cave, and in a small square room is the lingam which is the emblem of Śiva. Most remarkable of all the Brahmanical excavations is the Kailasa Temple. This is not a subterranean cave but an actual temple cut out of the rock of the sloping hillside and left standing free in the midst of the pit from which it was quarried. The wall of the pit is over 100 feet deep at the back, and the court surrounding the temple is 280 feet long and 160 feet wide. It is estimated that 200,000 tons of stone were removed in the course of the excavations. There is a gateway, a two-storied porch, another entrance way, a hall with sixteen massive square columns, a dark inner shrine, and a pyramidal roof rising to a height of ninety-six feet. The basement on which the temple stands is carved with magnificent elephants and monsters, and there are innumerable sculptures all over the temple and in the corridors round the sides of the excavation. Specially featured is the god Śiva with his wife Parvati in their retreat on the sacred Mount Kailasa, after which the whole temple is named. Dating probably from the eighth century A.D., the Kailasa Temple has been called "the noblest Hindu memorial of ancient India." Of the Jaina caves, dating from the eighth to the thirteenth century, the earliest is probably the Indra Sabha. In the courtyard of this sanctuary there is a great rock elephant, and a monolithic column now fallen, then a square porch, and after that there are two halls cut into the hillside one above the other. On the walls and in the many compartments and shrines there are relief carvings and statues of the great Jaina ascetics and heroes, especially Parśva, Mahavira, and Gommata.

Even more famous Jaina monuments are to be found at Śatrunjaya and Mount Abu in western India. In each case the Jains selected a striking mountain and built upon it a veritable temple city. At Śatrunjaya there are over five hundred temples which date from the eleventh century to modern times, and more than six thousand separate statues of the Tirthankaras who were the founders of the Jaina faith. At Mount Abu two temples of the eleventh and thirteenth centuries are of outstanding beauty. Built of white marble, their doorways, pillars, ceilings, panels, and niches are carved with the most intricate designs. In many cases the marble is so thin that it is translucent. Much of the work is so delicate that it could not have been accomplished by ordinary chiseling but was done by scraping the marble away, and it is said that the masons were paid by the amount of marble which they removed in this manner.

At Khajuraho in Central India there are thirty temples, one-third of them Jaina, two-thirds Hindu, but all much alike in architecture and all dating around A.D. 1000. The Kandarya Mahadeva is a shrine of Śiva. Its tower rises to one hundred and sixteen feet above the ground and is so designed that the impression of height is very striking. Over eight hundred statues have been counted in the decoration of the temple. In Orissa there are notable temples at Bhubaneswar, Puri, and Konarak. The Lingaraja Temple at Bhubaneswar, built about A.D. 1000, with a tower one hundred and eighty feet high, has been called "perhaps the most majestic Indian temple now standing." Every inch of the surface is covered with carvings of the most elaborate sort, but non-Hindus are not allowed within the temple enclosure so it is not possible to get a close view. The Temple of Jagannath at Puri, a century or so later in date, is famous for the annual procession in which the images of the god and of his brother and sister are taken out in their cars and drawn through the pilgrim-crowded streets of the city. The Black Pagoda at Konarak, of about the same date but only partially preserved, bears carvings of wheels and horses which show that it was built to represent the chariot of the sun god. At Madura in South India there is the Great Temple which is held by some to be the finest and most representative of all Hindu temples, and it is truly impressive with its enormous size, great terraced towers, and remarkable hall of one thousand pillars (997 to be exact), but having been built for the most part in the seventeenth century it is considerably later than the other monuments to which we have here directed attention.

6 Prophets

of a New Day

The story of how India attained independence is in the first instance the story of Gandhi. Gandhi was a saint—to that fact millions of people testified as they bestowed upon him the title Mahatma, meaning "great soul." He was also a political power of the first magnitude. To the Western mind this combination seems strange, since in the West it has often been declared that the era of the saint has passed, and it has usually been supposed that a saint could not be effective in the world as it is anyway. Nevertheless Gandhi was both a man of the spirit and a man of politics. To him the search for God required action in the world, and activity in the world derived its guidance and effectiveness from the resources of religion. "Politics without religion," he said, "is dead."

Mohandas Karamchand Gandhi was born in Porbandar in Western India on October 2, 1869, a member of the Vaisya caste, the youngest of his father's six children and a son of his father's fourth wife. In accordance with the Hindu custom where the family arranges the marriages of the children at a very young age, he was wedded when thirteen years old to a girl of the same age. Her name was Kasturbai, she was a complete stranger to him, and entirely illiterate, yet she became not only the mother of their children but also a faithful and courageous fellow participant in Gandhi's political struggles, and when she died in 1944, the Mahatma wept her passing with genuine sorrow.

Shortly before his eighteenth birthday, Gandhi sailed for England where he studied law for four years. Returning to India, he made little progress in the legal profession at home, and when the opportunity arose to go to South Africa as a lawyer for a Muslim merchant firm he availed himself of it and went there. In South Africa there was a large number of Indian immigrants, many of them common laborers, and Gandhi found that they were the objects and victims of very strong racial prejudice. He himself suffered frequent indignities because of his race, being refused a room in a hotel, put off a train where he ventured to ride first-class, and beaten on a stagecoach for failure to do what a white man told him. Gandhi soon began to talk to his fellow countrymen about these abuses, and became their recognized leader in an effort for amelioration. So engrossed did he become in this endeavor that while he had intended to stay in South Africa one year, he remained more than twenty.

In South Africa, Gandhi developed some of his leading ideas and techniques of action. He urged his fellow countrymen to unite as Indians in spite of their differences as Hindus, Muslims, Parsis, or Christians, and to fight together for redress of their grievances. He organized an Indian Congress patterned after the Indian National Congress which already existed at home. He published a weekly paper and wrote pamphlets which were widely circulated. He organized cooperative settlements where he and like-minded persons lived together and did their own work, even that of the most menial sort. In protest against a poll tax which worked a great hardship on Indian laborers, he led a march of six thousand men, all pledged to endure anything which befell them, flogging, imprisonment, or death, without fighting back by any kind of physical violence. To this method of nonviolent struggle Gandhi gave the name of *satyagraha*, from

75

satya, "truth," and *agraha,* "force." By the application of such "truth-force" Gandhi won remarkable victories and, by the time he left South Africa, saw removed some of the worst abuses under which the Indians had suffered there.

In 1915 Gandhi came back to India to find himself a national figure on account of what he had done in South Africa. He did not, however, plunge into public affairs but pledged himself to keep silence on such matters for a full year. During that time he established a small cooperative settlement at Ahmedabad which he called the Satyagraha Ashram. He took into this Ashram a family of untouchables, and eventually adopted the untouchable daughter as his own. To the untouchables he gave the name of Harijans or "children of God." He also led his group in learning to do hand spinning so that they could clothe themselves by their own efforts. He made homespun cloth a symbol of self-sufficiency and came to feel that self-sufficiency would in turn lead to self-government.

The struggle for self-government took form only slowly. At the end of World War I the British government passed certain laws aimed at stricter control of sedition in India, and these appeared so harsh that they aroused a storm of resentment. Gandhi called for the holding of a hartal, that is a day of national mourning, fasting, and prayer. The observance was marred, however, by outbreaks of violence on the part of both his own followers and the officers of the government and, instead of proceeding with Satyagraha, Gandhi suspended the movement, declaring that the people were not yet ready for it. Later he and the Indian National Congress agreed upon a program of "progressive nonviolent non-cooperation" explicitly aimed at self-rule for India, preferably within the British Empire but outside it if necessary. Again, however, Gandhi called this off after a time because some of his own people committed murders. In spite of his halting of the campaign, the Mahatma was tried for exciting disaffection toward the government and sentenced to six years in jail, an imprisonment from which he was released after two years.

Finally Gandhi and the Indian National Congress determined upon a stand for the complete independence of India. On Independence

76

Day, January 26, 1930, millions of Indians took a pledge which echoed the American Declaration of Independence:

> We believe that it is the inalienable right of the Indian people, as of any other people, to have freedom and to enjoy the fruits of their toil and have the necessities of life, so that they may have full opportunities of growth. We believe also that if any government deprives a people of these rights and oppresses them the people have a further right to alter it or abolish it. The British Government in India has not only deprived the Indian people of their freedom but has based itself on the exploitation of the masses, and has ruined India economically, politically, culturally, and spiritually. We believe, therefore, that India must sever the British connection and attain complete independence.

The momentous declaration went on to state that the people would thenceforward prepare for civil disobedience and for the nonpayment of taxes. One of the most hated impositions was the salt tax which burdened every family. Gandhi attacked this by marching on foot to the sea, followed by immense throngs, and there, in symbolic defiance of the government monopoly, manufacturing a small amount of salt out of the ocean water. This set off a tremendous wave of acts of civil disobedience throughout India. The collection of taxes was resisted, British goods were boycotted, and business was brought almost to a standstill. When the police charged upon their groups, Gandhi's followers for the most part took the blows which fell without making any resistance, and when they were arrested and condemned to prison they went without complaint. Gandhi himself was returned to jail with probably one hundred thousand persons.

From this point on there could be little doubt that India would attain freedom in some form, but the actual negotiations leading to it were still long and involved, and Gandhi and thousands of his followers were in and out of prison repeatedly before it was achieved. At the same time a rift grew steadily deeper among Indian patriots, which Gandhi did his best to overcome but which led at last to the division of India in the very hour when independence was won. This was the separation between the Muslim League and the National Congress. The Muslim League was founded in 1906 as the counterpart and rival of the National Congress. Now, under the leadership of Mohammed Ali Jinnah, it took an increasingly vigorous part in political affairs. Jinnah and his associates contended that, in a free

India dominated by the Hindu majority, Muslims would not have the rights they should and that, accordingly, it was necessary to form a separate Muslim state. For his part, Gandhi's position was expressed in his famous plea to Jinnah, "You can cut me in two, but don't cut India in two."

So powerful did the Muslim pressure become, however, that in the end Gandhi had to accept the partition of India. When the free and separate dominions of India and Pakistan came into being on August 15, 1947, he observed the day only in silence and prayer. During the years of struggle between the two sides in this controversy, the fears and hatreds of both Hindus and Muslims had been intensified. Before partition and especially after it, great violence broke out between the two parties. When the two separate states were established, millions of Hindus fled in terror from Pakistan and millions of Muslims from India, and in the riots which took place at this time some 1,500,000 persons were killed. In the face of this terrible carnage, as a form of penance for it, and as the only way he knew to try to bring a new spirit into Hindu-Muslim relations, Gandhi undertook a fast. For six days the frail little man voluntarily refrained from all sustenance until finally, as he grew weaker and weaker, leaders of both Hindus and Muslims came to him with such pledges of amity that he was satisfied. Less than two weeks later, as he walked in to his evening prayer meeting in the grounds of Birla House in New Delhi, Gandhi was assassinated by a Hindu extremist. It was January 30, 1948, and Gandhi was seventy-eight years of age.

There is no doubt that the primary inspiration of Gandhi's life was derived from Hinduism. To him "the supreme book for the knowledge of truth" was the Bhagavad Gita, which he read first as a student in England. It is the teaching of this classical Hindu work that while renunciation and mystic contemplation have their place, the superior way which leads to salvation is that of selfless activity in the world. Although he desired to reform Hinduism at such points as the treatment of untouchables, he never broke away from the fundamental structure and ideas of the religion. This adherence was symbolized by a remark he made to an American visitor only a few days before his death in which he spoke of himself as "a cow-lover." Along with Hinduism, Christianity, particularly the teachings of the Sermon on the Mount with which he became acquainted while in England, influenced him in the formation of his philosophy. Two Christian hymns were also favorites of his, "Lead, Kindly Light," and "When I Survey the Wondrous Cross." It was Gandhi's desire, indeed, to open his life to truth from every side, yet always to pursue a course in line with his own fundamental convictions. He said, "I do not want my house to be walled in on all sides and my windows to be stuffed. I want cultures of all lands to be blown about my house as freely as possible. But I refuse to be blown off my feet by any."

Jawaharlal Nehru, Gandhi's successor as the leader of India, was born in Allahabad on November 14, 1889, a member of the Brahman caste and a descendant of a Kashmiri family. His father, Motilal, was a prosperous lawyer, and the family home was large and fine. Nehru had two sisters, Swarup and Krishna. Swarup was to become Mrs. Vijaya Lakshmi Pandit who led the Indian delegation to the General Assembly of the United Nations, and served as Indian High Commissioner to London. Jawaharlal was raised to be at home in both Indian and English customs, and at fifteen was taken to England to school. He stayed there seven years, going to school first at Harrow, then studying at Cambridge and at London. At home in India again, he was wedded to Kamala, a Kashmiri girl of seventeen, and to them a daughter, Indira, was born.

Interesting himself in political matters, Jawaharlal joined the Moderates of the Indian National Congress, the group which believed in cooperating with the British government and to which his father already belonged. However, as he became acquainted with Gandhi, a frequent guest in the Nehru home, Jawaharlal moved rapidly toward acceptance of the movement for national independence, and in time Motilal came to share many of the same views. From 1920 on, both father and son were committed to Gandhi's cause.

Wanting to learn their real situation, Jawaharlal Nehru began to travel among the peasants throughout India. As he addressed them in meeting after meeting, he felt that he was finding his proper place

of service and leadership. By the end of 1921 both he and his father were sentenced to jail on account of their activities. Set free after three months, Jawaharlal was present at the trial when Gandhi received his sentence of six years' imprisonment; a few weeks later he himself was arrested again and returned to custody. Thus began that series of imprisonments during which Nehru spent a total of sixteen years in jail.

In 1927 the Nehru family was invited to visit Moscow on the occasion of the celebration of the tenth anniversary of the Russian Revolution. Jawaharlal thought that he sensed a great determination of spirit among the peasants of the land and felt that in many ways their cause and that of his own people at home were the same. In 1928 Motilal Nehru was president of the Indian National Congress as he had been before, in 1929 Jawaharlal was elected at Gandhi's suggestion, and father passed to son the gavel of leadership. Thus Jawaharlal headed the Congress at the time when the pledge of

national independence was formulated and taken. In the stern days of civil disobedience following Gandhi's salt march, both Jawaharlal and his father were again in jail, but Motilal was soon let out because of poor health and early in 1931 he passed away. Jawaharlal's wife Kamala also fell sick and after protracted illness died in 1936. Two years later his mother also departed from this life. Confined much of this time to prison and burdened with anxiety concerning these personal matters as well as for the cause of independence, Nehru wrote. Between 1930 and 1933 he penned a series of letters to his daughter Indira which were published as *Glimpses of World History* (1942); after that he wrote his autobiography which appeared in 1941 under the title *Toward Freedom*.

As the struggle for freedom went on, it became increasingly evident that Gandhi's mantle would fall upon Nehru's shoulders. The two men were by no means always in agreement. The occasions on which Gandhi suddenly suspended Satyagraha dismayed Nehru; the master's preoccupation with the spinning wheel seemed out of place to his follower who believed that in the modern world the development of modern industry was necessary; and the Mahatma's mingling of religion and politics was not in line with the more secular tendency of the younger man's mind. Yet in spite of the times when Nehru felt himself estranged from the great leader, he always returned to his loyalty to him, and until today speaks of Gandhi as the chief inspiration of his work.

When independence came, then, it was Nehru who was chosen to head the new India. At first India remained a dominion in the British Commonwealth of Nations, which meant that the land was under a governor general appointed by the king of England. The governor general was advised by an Indian cabinet, however, and the prime minister in this cabinet was Jawaharlal Nehru. He continued in the same position when, with the adoption of its constitution on January 26, 1950, India, although still related to the British Commonwealth of Nations, became a sovereign and independent republic.[1]

As prime minister, Nehru has labored indefatigably to build a new India. Writing of the period when he was in the midst of his work for independence, he said, "I passed through this vast country like some hurricane." In those times he went not only by airplane and railway and automobile but also by elephant, camel, horse, steamer, canoe, bicycle, and on foot. On one day his first meeting was at eight o'clock in the morning and his last, seven hours late, at four o'clock the next morning, and during the day he traveled four hundred and fifteen miles. He still travels almost constantly and works very hard. As when he first went among the peasants to learn of their problems firsthand, he seems to want to see each critical situation for himself. When there is famine in the south, another refugee influx in the east, unrest in the north, misunderstanding among the hill tribes; he goes there immediately and talks to and with the people. Simply following the daily reports of his travels and addresses during my time in India enabled me to see that Nehru was still a very hard-working

[1] Pakistan remained longer in the dominion status, but a Constituent Assembly has drafted a constitution which, it was reported in February, 1955, will soon be adopted and will make Pakistan an independent "Islamic republic." Although an elected president will replace the governor general hitherto appointed by the British monarch, Pakistan will remain within the British Commonwealth of Nations, just as India has done.

man. On November 14, 1952, Nehru celebrated his sixty-third birthday. At that time a writer in India described him thus: "At sixty-three Mr. Nehru does not look a bit older than he was last year or the year before. He still walks along the corridors of Parliament House and the Central Secretariat with the briskness and agility of a man of thirty and retains the restlessness and impatience which come from physical and mental energy. If he ever feels the effects of age and the strain of endless work, he does not show it." The same observer noted that during the preceding year the only disability Nehru suffered was a sprained leg and this happened in Parliament House when he was making an effort to reach the Chamber without delay. "Work," the correspondent concluded, "—usually eighteen hours in the twenty-four—remains the prime minister's main occupation in life."[1]

In October, 1954, it was reported that Nehru had spoken of being tired and was considering passing on the prime ministership to Morarji Desaii, chief minister of Bombay state and treasurer of the Congress party. This report was discounted, however, by the interpretation which held that Mr. Nehru was only making a gesture aimed at keeping dissidents within his party in line. In November, 1954, it was further reported that the working committee of the Indian National Congress had nominated Uchharang Rai N. Dhebar, chief minister of Saurashtra and a loyal follower of Nehru, to succeed him as Chairman of the party, but had rejected as "inconceivable" any suggestion that Nehru relinquish the prime ministership.

Wherever Nehru goes he is greeted by large crowds, and at least some of the loyalty which the people of India used to have for Gandhi has been transferred to him. On a recent visit to the tribal people of Assam, a large group of costumed boys and girls performed a traditional dance for him. The content and significance given to the ritual were new, however, for the children sang the praises of "Uncle Jawahar and Father Gandhi." Prosaically translated from the Abor language, the song of the children went as follows: "On this bright day let us dance as our Uncle Jawahar has come. India has got independence through Father Gandhi of Delhi who was the highest of

---

[1] *The Statesman* (Calcutta) Nov. 15, 1952

all but who used to put his dhoti down to his knees only [a sign of no pretension]. By the struggles of Uncle Jawahar and Father Gandhi, India has obtained independence and every Indian is progressing. Let us march with the other people of India." At another place a little old lady waited many hours with a small cup of milk in her hand, and Nehru stopped and smilingly received it from her. Such spontaneous acts of affection meet him everywhere and testify to the devotion of multitudes of Indian people to Gandhi's successor and their present leader.

In earlier days Nehru declared his belief in socialism very plainly. In an address to the Indian National Congress he once declared: "I see no way of ending poverty, the vast unemployment, the degradation and the subjection of the Indian people except through socialism. . . . That means the ending of private property, except in a restricted sense, and the replacement of the present profit system by a higher ideal of cooperative service." If that has remained his goal, at any rate Nehru has moved toward it slowly, cautiously, and with consideration of the rights and opinions of others. In conversation with an American visitor in 1951, when Nehru was asked whether he believed that basically the state was created to advance the welfare of the individual, he replied, "Undoubtedly." He went on to declare that in his own thinking the individual was uppermost, yet that the rights of the individual had also to be balanced by the obligations of the individual to the social organism. In the modern world, he thought, it was not possible to escape centralized authority, and he saw the state as having the duty not only to protect the individual from foreign enemies or internal disorders, but also to provide him with opportunities of progress, including education, health, sanitation, and everything that would enable him to fit himself for the work he was capable of doing. To accomplish these ends it appeared to him inevitable that there would be a large measure of centralization, yet he insisted upon a desire to keep this centralization at a minimum and to decentralize as many enterprises as possible. In an address delivered at Nagpur on October 31, 1952, Nehru declared that the major problem of India was that of ending poverty and unemployment, and building up a classless society based on equality of opportunity. In pointing to how India could make progress toward this goal, he insisted that the foremost need was for everyone to work hard and appreciate the dignity of labor; that all should endeavor to produce more wealth by increasing production whether in the field or in the factory; that the wealth so produced should be properly distributed; and that there were no short cuts to prosperity, for India could not afford to undergo the trials and tribulations of certain countries which have sought to achieve their goal through revolutions.

As far as religion is concerned, Nehru tells in his writings how the spectacle of what is called religion in India and elsewhere has filled him with horror. It has seemed to him to stand almost always for blind belief, reaction, dogma, bigotry, superstition, and exploitation. He has often wished to make a clean sweep of it. He has noticed that there is something else in it, however, something which answers a deep craving of human beings, something which brings peace and comfort to multitudes of people. Yet for himself he says, "I am afraid it is impossible for me to seek anchorage in this way. I prefer the open sea with all its storms and tempests." Nevertheless, there

is certainly in his mind a sense of what is everlasting and ultimate, and of which the mountains have often been to him a symbol.

There were many who cannot be told of here who worked with Gandhi to make India free and who have worked with Nehru to shape the new state, but one architect of the emerging structure of India's future must be mentioned. This is Bhimrao Ramji Ambedkar, who was born on April 14, 1893. His family belonged to the untouchables, and he grew up in poverty. Then, however, the ruler of the native state of Baroda noticed him, paid for his education in India, and sent him to the United States to study. In 1916 Ambedkar received the Ph.D. degree from Columbia University. After that he also studied in England at the London School of Economics and in Germany at the University of Bonn. When he returned to India in 1924, he established himself as a lawyer in Bombay and attained success and distinction in spite of the strong opposition with which he was met by high-caste Hindus. Before long he became the recognized leader and spokesman of the untouchables, and represented them in conferences with the British government. Since Gandhi claimed that the Indian National Congress should speak for all India, and Ambedkar did not believe that it properly represented the untouchables, the two men were often in strong disagreement. So deeply did he feel about the oppressions to which the untouchables were subjected in orthodox Hinduism, that Ambedkar was reported at one time to be thinking of leading his community en masse into Christianity, at another into Islam. Nevertheless, when the time came to draft the constitution of free India, it was Ambedkar who wrote much of the document, even as he has also drafted the Hindu Code Bill still under debate. His published books have had to do with finance, with the partition of India, and with caste and untouchability. In his volume, *The Untouchables*, published in 1948, Dr. Ambedkar declared that the existence in India of criminal tribes, aboriginal tribes, and untouchables was an abomination, and that the Hindu civilization which had produced these three classes was "a diabolical contrivance to suppress and enslave humanity." In December, 1952, and January, 1953, speaking as the president of the All-India Scheduled Castes' Federation, which is the organization of the depressed classes,

Dr. Ambedkar said that the condition of his people had grown worse rather than better since independence and that there were not as many of them in government positions as there were during British rule. Predicting that the misery, starvation, and squalor of the Harijans would usher in "dreadful results" if their condition were not improved, he declared: "I shall wait for another couple of years, or even till the next elections, for the alleviation of the misery of my people, and if a new deal is not forthcoming through negotiations, I shall be forced to take recourse to stern measures, which might upset the chariot of the government, and anarchy might follow."

7 Progress

in Democracy

The constitution of the Union of India was made public in draft form in 1948, approved by a Constituent Assembly in 1949, and formally put in force on January 26, 1950, just twenty years after the original Indian pledge of independence. According to the constitution, India is a sovereign and democratic republic. The preamble states:

We, the people of India, having solemnly resolved to constitute India into a Sovereign Democratic Republic and to secure to all its citizens:
Justice, social, economic and political;
Liberty of thought, expression, belief, faith and worship;
Equality of status and opportunity; and to promote among them all
Fraternity assuring the dignity of the individual and the unity of the Nation;
. . . do hereby adopt, enact and give to ourselves this Constitution.

As I have heard Dr. S. Radhakrishnan, the vice-president of India, point out, this emphasis upon justice, liberty, equality, and fraternity discloses dependence upon political ideas which originated in France, England, and the United States of America, and shows that India has chosen to establish a form of government more akin to that of the Western democracies than any other.

In the actual organization of the government, a strong central authority is created and the states are given only limited powers as compared, for example, with the United States of America. The central government is empowered to pass legislation in any field which is in the national interest, and the president can suspend any state constitution. The setting up of the new central authority with the subordination to it of the multitudinous units into which India was previously divided was no small task. The princely states were a special problem. It was decided that there would have to be a grouping of many of the smaller units into larger bodies, and that the autocratic rule in the princely states would have to be replaced by democratic government. Sardar Vallabhbhai Patel took the lead in carrying out these arrangements. He was a strong nationalist and follower of Gandhi, who was often in prison in the days of civil disobedience. Under Nehru, he was deputy prime minister of India. He was recognized as a man of conservative views and until his death in 1950 wielded much influence. He went throughout India, working out the details of the integration of the states with the central government and arranging the generous pensions on which most of the princes were retired. The large princely state of Hyderabad constituted a special problem because the Nizam, as the ruler was called, wished to join neither India nor Pakistan. When severe Communist uprisings broke out there in 1948, the Indian army was sent in and the government was taken over. By 1950 it was possible to summarize what had been done. The following statistical statement suggests how complex the process was: 216 states were joined with what had been British provinces; 275 states were merged into new unions of states; and 61 states were brought under the direct administration of the central government.

In 1953 a new state of Andhra was formed. The basis of the state is linguistic. The people of the region speak the Telugu language, and for a long time there had been agitation among them to have their own political organization. In this agitation the Communists were active, but the climax came when a Gandhian leader named Potti Sriramulu perished in December, 1952, at the end of a 58-day "fast unto death" directed toward the same political end. This led to acceptance by the national government of the demands for the formation of the new state, but even as the decision was announced in January, 1953, many misgivings were also expressed as to what the action portended. It was pointed out, for example, that the neighboring state of Hyderabad was composed of eight Telugu, five Marathi, and three Kanarese districts, and thus was ideally constituted for a similar division which both Communists and many Congress members were said to desire. Such a linguistic movement, carried to its logical extreme, would fractionize India into more than two hundred separate states. Nevertheless, the announced decision was adhered to, and on October 1, 1953, Andhra State came into being. In inaugural ceremonies at the provisional capital of Kurnool, Nehru warned against irresponsible agitation for more linguistic states, but when he repeated the same plea in Madras, pro-Communist members of the Dravidian Progressive Federation waved black flags and shouted, "Nehru, go back!" Among the 146 members of the Legislative Assembly of Andhra State are forty Communists, a dozen Communist sympathizers, and only forty-one members of the Congress party. The Congress, the Praja Socialists, and other minor groups, were able to elect a Gandhian leader named Tangatura Prakasam as chief minister, but the Communist leader, Tadpatri Nagi Reddy, hopes soon to bring about the downfall of Prakasam and the establishment of the first Communist government in any Indian state. Early in March, 1955, however, the first reports from new state elections in Andhra indicated that an anti-Communist United Front led by Nehru's Congress Party had won an impressive victory over the Communists.

In 1954 the small French enclaves at Pondichéry, Karaikal, Mahe, and Yanam were at last given up by France, under Premier Pierre Mendès-France, to become a part of the Republic of India. The three colonies of Portugal, at Goa, Damao, and Diu, on the other hand, were still tightly held by the Portuguese government, in spite of increasing public agitation for their surrender to India. Kashmir continued under dispute between India and Pakistan, and this problem was made much more difficult from the point of view of India by the military assistance pact between the United States and Pakistan.

In its organization the central government of India has a parliament consisting of two houses. The lower body, known as the House of the People, has 500 members, elected by universal adult suffrage. The upper house is called the Council of States. It is made up of 250 members, who are elected by the lower houses of the state legislatures. The titular head of the state is a president who is elected for five years. In 1955 Dr. Rajendra Prasad holds this office. The president is advised by a cabinet and prime minister, and in actual fact, it is the prime minister, at present Mr. Nehru, who is the real head of India. There is a supreme court, composed of seven justices, which is charged with the duty of guarding and interpreting the fundamental law of the land. The constitution also contains a Statement of Fundamental Rights, in which the influence of the bill of rights of the United States of America may be recognized. This statement declares that no person shall be deprived of life or personal liberty except according to procedure established by law. It abolishes and forbids the practice of untouchability in any form. It states that no citizen may be denied

access to restaurants, hotels, or places of public resort on grounds only of religion, race, caste, or sex. It provides for freedom of worship and equality of treatment of all religions by the state. It guarantees freedom of speech, except that the government may make laws against anything which is offensive to decency or morality or which undermines security or tends to overthrow the state.

There is also found in the constitution a list of Directive Principles of State Policy which are not specific laws but rather goals toward which the government is expected to work. These call for an economic system which does not result in a concentration of wealth detrimental to the people, and which does not abuse the health and strength of men and women or the tender age of children; for equal pay for men and women for the same work; for benefits for old age, unemployment, and disability; and for free and compulsory education for all children under fourteen years of age.

In addition the constitution makes Hindi the official language of India, but allows the use of English for official purposes until 1965.

In fundamental structure, therefore, India has chosen to establish the framework of a democracy. The first general election was held in 1951-1952. On the basis of the new adult franchise which allows anyone who is twenty-one years of age and of sound mind to vote, 176,000,000 voters were eligible. Of that number about 45 per cent participated, although the percentage varied in different states. Since many of these were illiterate and had to vote for parties by recognizing their symbols, the very holding of such an election was an achievement of magnitude. Polling lasted for over 100 days.

Seventy-seven political parties were represented in the election, eight of them being nation-wide in scope. In the voting for the House of the People, the Indian National Congress received the largest number of votes, nearly 48,000,000 or 45 per cent of the total poll. The Congress party still has behind it the record of its long and successful struggle for the independence of India, and upon that much of its continuing prestige depends. In the heat of that struggle it was easy to blame all of India's ills upon the British and to suggest that a complete transformation of Indian life would accompany the attain-

ment of independence. That such an analysis and such a hope were not fully realistic is now evident. Reformation proved easier to promise than to accomplish. As the party in power, Congress has undoubtedly grown more and more conservative, and the fact that 55 out of every 100 voters in the recent election in effect voted against Congress suggests that its influence, while still great, is waning rather than increasing. As already noted, until recently Mr. Nehru has served as both chairman of the Congress party and prime minister of the country.

The Socialist party received the second largest number of votes, over 11,000,000 or 10 per cent of the total. This party broke away from the Indian National Congress after 1948, believing that it was necessary to proceed much more rapidly and directly with social reform than Congress was evidently disposed to do. Its leader was Jayaprakash P. Narain. He went to the United States for his higher education and worked his way through four schools, beginning with the University of California and finally obtaining the B.A. and M.A. degrees from Ohio State University. To that experience Narain credited his self-confidence and his different attitude toward labor.

93

He noted especially the contrast between the workingman in India who bowed and scraped before his master and the one in America who held his head high. In 1951 Acharya J. B. Kripalani, defeated for the presidency of the Congress, organized the Kisan Mazdoor Praja party to advocate among other aims the giving of the land to those who till it. In the general election this group received over 6,000,000 votes, nearly 6 per cent of the total. In 1952 they merged with the Socialists to form the Praja Socialist party. In addition to Narain and Kripalani, Asoka Mehta and Rammanohar Lohia are contemporary leaders. Proposing to alter the very structure of Indian society, the Praja Socialist party stands for equalization of wealth, elimination of luxuries and waste, full employment, economic planning, and social mobility. It calls for nationalization of major industry, promotion of cooperatives, trade unions, and consumers' groups, and encouragement of panchayats or village councils "as the chief organs of functional democracy." It believes in going ahead immediately with land reform, and its representatives engage heartily in village improvement work. In a pamphlet on *Indian Political Parties* published in 1948 by the All-India Congress Committee, N. V. Rajkumar, secretary of the Foreign Department of the Committee, wrote: "To the average citizen the Socialist Party appears as an embodiment of all those hopes and aspirations which freedom was to bring in its wake." In his booklet on *The Political Mind of India* published in 1952, Asoka Mehta asserted that the first prerequisite of progress was "clarity against capitalism and communism." Refusing to oscillate between the two, much less to give allegiance to one in practice and the other in theory as the Congress party does, the Socialists, he said, have unveiled the visages of both the ideologies and shown the affinities which unite them as the twin products of the industrial revolution. Maintaining that the ultimate challenge to communism and capitalism has to be in the realm of ideas, he declared: "The Socialist Party's one achievement has been to sail forth boldly to ideological clarity." On the basis of many conversations, it was my own impression that the majority of the young people of India in particular are strongly socialist in their thinking today.

In the 1951-1952 general election the Communist and allied parties were supported by over 5,000,000 voters, 5 per cent of the total. The Communist party has been active in India for nearly thirty years; in 1951 it was stated that the party membership had never exceeded 100,000. The current program of the party usually follows the line laid down in Moscow and the ultimate aim would therefore appear to be to tie India closely to Russia. The Communist leader, P. C. Joshi, edits a periodical called *India To-day* which is constantly filled with articles of the most violent sort, following exactly the line of Russian propaganda. For example, in the issue of August, 1952, Joshi described the United States of America as "the imperialist over-lord of the Atlantic and Pacific Alliances, with its strategic bases girdling round the world, its economic claws reaching out to every country that can be pressured into asking for economic aid," and wrote as follows concerning international affairs, "As after World War I, imperialist aggressive drive has been launched in Asia to retain it as the colonial hinterland of the imperialist West, to prevent its peoples achieving their national liberation and to win bridgeheads, strategic bases, material resources and manpower for World War III to reconquer what is now the anti-imperialist People's World, stretching from Peking to Berlin, covering one-third of the globe, at whose head stands the mighty U.S.S.R. constructing great projects of Communism." The Communist newspaper *Blitz*, which calls itself "Asia's Foremost Newsmagazine," is sold regularly on the streets of Indian cities. It is written in the crudest and most scurrilous fashion. For several examples of its favorite topics I may cite the issue of November 29, 1952, in which there was an attack on the greed for power and scramble for office in the Indian National Congress, a statement that the American wheat sent to India consisted of cattle fodder unfit for human consumption, and a panegyric on Moscow as the place where the people enjoy the fruits of their labor. Communist books are sold on the streets in Indian cities at very low prices, movies like "The Battle of Stalingrad" depicting the Russians' "finest hour" are screened, and radio broadcasts come in regularly from the powerful station at Tashkent.

The four groups just mentioned, the Congress, Socialist, Praja, and Communist parties, were the unquestioned leaders in the 1951-1952 general election and the only ones to receive more than 5,000,000 votes each. Today, concentrated into three groups by the merger of the Socialist and Praja parties, they are still the most important factors in the Indian political scene. Next there are three communal parties of nation-wide scope, the Jan Sangh, the Ram Rajya Parishad, and the Akhil Bharat Hindu Mahasabha. Like the Muslim League which contended for Muslim rights and gained its objective with the formation of the separate state of Pakistan, these parties claim to stand for the special interests of the Hindu community. Organized by Shyamaprasad Mookerji, vice-chancellor of the University of Calcutta, the Jan Sangh polled over 3,000,000 votes, 3 per cent of the total in the 1951-1952 election. It has been concerned for the Hindu minority in Pakistan and has wished either to reunite India or to further divide Eastern Pakistan. In the summer of 1953 Dr. Mookerji died of a heart attack while under arrest in Kashmir where he had deliberately gone without a permit in order to dramatize his contention that Kashmir belongs to India. The Ram Rajya Parishad secured over 2,000,000 votes, almost 2 per cent of the total poll. It has been described as "the die-hard party of the status quo." It opposes the Hindu Code Bill and seeks to assure the fullest safeguards for property rights. The Hindu Mahasabha or Great Society of Hindus was founded in 1923 at Banaras by Pandit Malaviya, and took a prominent part in the controversy with the Muslim League. At that time it declared that "India belongs to the Hindus and is nobody else's patrimony." In the 1951-1952 election it secured over 1,000,000 votes, almost 1 per cent of the total. The Mahasabha believes in the maintenance of the caste system and the preservation of orthodox Hinduism. At the beginning of 1953 it was emphasizing the problems of Indo-Pakistani relations in general and of Kashmir in particular, and was also spending much time on its favorite topic of cow protection, the position of the party being that a national law should be passed banning all slaughter of cows. At this time the president of the organization was N. C. Chatterjee.

The list of the eight parties of national scope in the 1951-1952 election is completed with the Scheduled Castes' Federation. This is the organization of the depressed classes, already mentioned in the preceding chapter, of which Dr. Ambedkar is president. In the general election the Federation received 2,500,000 votes, over 2 per cent of the total.

Among the many other parties of more limited scope we will refer only to the Shiromani Akali Dal, which is the organization of the Sikhs. In the election more than 1,000,000 votes were cast for the party, slightly more than 1 per cent of the total. In the days before independence the Akali Dal fought vigorously for Sikh rights, now it claims that "the lot of the Sikhs has particularly worsened. They have been suppressed, maligned and otherwise treated as undesirable aliens in their very homeland." As a solution to the problem the party urges that the Sikhs should have a separate Punjabi-speaking state of their own within the Indian republic. On December 27, 1953, Sikhs of the Akali Dal were reported to have denounced Nehru over this issue in one of the most violent demonstrations against him in his entire career. The prime minister had gone to the vicinity of Patiala to speak at a famous Sikh place of worship, but was met by hundreds of Sikhs brandishing sticks, spears, and axes, and shouting anti-Nehru slogans. Although introduced by the Maharaja of Patiala, Nehru was unable to speak more than a few words when the tumult broke out again. When the Akali leader, Tara Singh, refused to quiet the demonstration and declared that Nehru could not speak there, the prime minister, the maharaja, and their party were forced to withdraw.

Now turning again to the party presently in power, the Congress leadership has expressed itself strongly in recent days about both the extreme right and extreme left in the political scene. Concerning the Hindu Mahasabha, Mr. Nehru says that by arousing religious feelings they are making a mischievous effort to serve their own political purposes, that by inciting communal[1] hatred they are diverting attention from fundamental economic problems, and that if they continue to create disruption and to indulge in misguidance of the people they will have to be dealt with by strict measures. With regard to the Communists the prime minister declares that they seem to function on the principle that if they break up everything, something will come out of the wreck. He expresses appreciation of much that the Communists have done economically, but emphasizes that in practice they concentrate on destructive activity. Of their disruptive methods he said in January, 1953: "I am of the firm opinion that if this method of

[1]The terms communal and communalism are used in India with reference to a society of separated religious or caste groups.

98

violence is adopted, it will ruin the country and bring civil war—and all progress will be stopped." As to the relationship of the Congress party and the Socialists there is more obscurity than light. Recalling Nehru's one-time outright espousal of socialist doctrine it would seem as if the two groups would have much in common. Taking Mehta's very strong attack on Congress, from which quotation was given above, as typical of Socialist opinion, it would seem as if the possibility of *rapprochement* were very slight. At the beginning of 1953 the press carried stories of a proposed meeting between Mr. Nehru and Mr. Narain at which a possible merging of the Socialist party in the Indian National Congress would be discussed. Both Narain and Kripalani were credited with statements that there was no special ideological difference between their party and the Congress, and a letter from Narain to Nehru was quoted in which the former assured the prime minister that he and his party "were always prepared to cooperate" in fighting communalism. For the present the two parties seem to be going their separate ways, and Narain is reported devoting himself to village improvement and land reform work. There are many, however, who believe that only some kind of increased cooperation between the Congress and the Socialist party will make it possible for the government to work more effectively for reform and progress than it has yet done and thereby to resist more positively the threats from the Mahasabha and others of their kind on the one hand and from the Communists and their confreres on the other. Narain himself is often spoken of as a possible successor to Nehru.

8 Problems of Population, Economics, and Social Life

VIII. Problems of Population, Economics, and Social Life

Figures on the population of India are available from the Indian census. The making of a decennial enumeration was begun under British rule, and the first census was taken in 1871. The initial attempt was limited in scope and success, thus the first relatively full and dependable statistics come from 1881. Since the census has been taken every ten years, the most recent enumeration was in 1951, which was the first census since freedom and partition. In undertaking statistical comparisons it must therefore be remembered that the previous censuses covered what is now Pakistan and India both, while the last Indian census was of course limited to India alone. That the taking of such a census is itself an undertaking of great magnitude may be realized when it is noted that in 1951, 600,000 enumerators visited 64,000,000 homes in order to compile the necessary records. The state of Jammu and Kashmir and the tribal areas of Assam were not included in the 1951 census.[1]

---

[1] For figures up through the census of 1941 see Kingsley Davis, *The Population of India* (Princeton: Princeton University Press, 1951). At the present writing the results of the 1951 census have not yet been completely published. 1951 census figures in this chapter are drawn from the *Monthly Abstract of Statistics*, published by the Central Statistical Organization of the Government of India in New Delhi, Volume 6, Number 7, July 1953, pp. 1-3; and *The Indian and Pakistan Year Book and Who's Who 1952-1953*, Volume XXXVIII, edited by Frank Moraes, published by The Times of India, Bombay, Delhi, and Calcutta, pp. 9f.

In 1951 the total population of India exclusive of Jammu and Kashmir and the tribal areas of Assam was registered as 356,829,485, with 183,305,654 males and 173,523,831 females. It was estimated that the population of Jammu and Kashmir was 4,410,000, and of the tribal areas of Assam 560,631. Adding these figures gives a grand total of 361,800,116. The area of India including Assam is 1,176,860 square miles; that of Jammu and Kashmir is 92,780 square miles; all together this makes a grand total of 1,269,640 square miles. An over-all population density of 285 persons per square mile is therefore indicated. In different parts of the country, however, there is much variation. West Bengal has 24,810,308 people in an area of 30,775 square miles, or 806 per square mile; Rajasthan has a population of 15,290,797 in 130,207 square miles, or 117 per square mile; and in the inhospitable wastes of Kutch there are 567,606 people in 16,724 square miles, or 34 per square mile.

Compared with a world population estimated at 2,386,810,000, the population of India represents 15.1 per cent of the total and is second only to China which with 462,277,637 persons accounts for 19.4 per cent of the total. China, however, with 3,290,926 square miles, has a land area two and one-half times as great as India. Compared with the United States which had a population of 150,697,361 in 1950 and has a land area of 3,022,387 square miles, India has more than twice the number of people in less than half the amount of territory. On the other hand, there are population densities in excess of that of India in a number of other lands. Italy has 401 persons per square mile, Germany 468, Japan 571, England 799, and Java 814. But in most of these countries industry and trade make much larger contributions to the wealth of the people than in India, and it is therefore only in such places as Java and perhaps Japan that there is a heavier pressure of the population upon the land than in India.

Official reports on the birth rate in India give the following figures per thousand population in the years since partition: 1948, 25.2; 1949, 26.4; 1950, 24.8; 1951, 24.9; 1952, 28.1; which makes an average of 25.88. This compares with a reported 33.3 in 1938. There is reason to think, however, that many births go unregistered in India, and some estimates of the birth rate run as high as 35 or

36 per thousand. In the United States the birth rate was 17.6 in 1938, and since 1948 has averaged almost exactly 24. Likewise the Indian death rate per thousand population is reported as follows for the same years: 1948, 17.0; 1949, 15.8; 1950, 16.0; 1951, 14.2; 1952, 14.4; or an average of 15.5. In 1938 the figure was 23.7. Again some estimates place the death rate much higher and suppose that there are actually as many as 33 deaths per thousand. In the United States the death rate was 10.6 in 1938, and since 1948 has averaged 9.7. It must be concluded, therefore, that both by the recorded figures and yet more by the realistic estimates which run in excess of them, there is a very high birth rate and also a very high death rate in India. According to the 1951 census, however, the life expectancy has been increasing markedly and stands now at 32 years. Thus, an Indian born now has a life expectancy five years longer than one born in 1941 and ten years longer than one born in 1931.

The actual growth of the population of the subcontinent for the census periods from 1881 to 1941 is shown in the following table:

Year	Population	Increase	
		Net	Percentage
1881	250,125,000		
1891	279,548,000	22,471,000	9.0
1901	283,827,000	4,278,000	1.5
1911	302,995,000	16,169,000	6.8
1921	305,674,000	2,679,000	0.9
1931	338,119,000	32,445,000	10.6
1941	388,800,000	50,681,000	15.0

In the sixty years covered by this table the total increase in population was 43.8 per cent. For a seventy-year period ending in 1941 the population may be estimated to have increased about 54 per cent. During the same seventy years the population of the United Kingdom increased 56 per cent; that of Japan about 136 per cent.

In 1951 the population of India proper was, as we have seen, 356,829,485. The figure for the corresponding area in 1941 was approximately 314,830,000. For this decade, therefore, the increase was 41,999,485, or 13.3 per cent. In the United States the popula-

102

tion was 150,697,361 in 1950, and 131,669,275 in 1940. Thus there was an increase here of 19,028,086, or 14.5 per cent.

These figures show, accordingly, that the present rate of growth of the Indian population is not in excess of that of many other lands. It is the absolute growth rather than the percentage of increase which is most massive. Calculated on the basis of a total population of 361,000,000, a 13.3 per cent increase in the present decade will add over 48,000,000 persons by 1961. That is more than the entire popu-

lation of England, France, or Italy. If this rate of increase is maintained, the population of India will be approximately 675,000,000 in A.D. 2001.

Of the entire poulation of India about 15 per cent is classified as urban, 85 per cent as rural. An area is usually considered rural if its population does not exceed 5,000; a town has more than 5,000 people; and a city has 100,000 or more. According to the 1951 census there were five cities in India with a population of over one million:

Greater Calcutta	4,550,117
Bombay	2,840,011
Delhi	1,743,992
Madras	1,429,985
Hyderabad with Secunderabad	1,085,074

Sixty-eight more cities had over 100,000 inhabitants. There were 700,000 villages.

In the same census the population of India proper, excluding 135,096 persons in the Punjab for whom details were not available, was divided according to categories of livelihood. In this division 249,122,449 persons were classed as agricultural, 107,571,940 as nonagricultural. The more detailed tabulation in this regard was as follows:

Livelihood Categories	Male	Female	Total
I. Agricultural	126,205,686	122,916,763	249,122,449
Cultivators of land wholly or mainly owned, and their dependents	85,115,449	82,231,052	167,346,501
Cultivators of land wholly or mainly unowned, and their dependents	16,256,195	15,383,424	31,639,719
Cultivating laborers and their dependents	22,395,852	22,416,076	44,811,928
Noncultivating owners of land, agricultural rent receivers, and their dependents	2,438,190	2,886,111	5,324,301
II. Nonagricultural	57,028,733	50,543,207	107,571,940
Production other than cultivation	20,024,164	17,636,033	37,660,197
Commerce	11,232,253	10,076,618	21,308,871
Transport	3,114,358	2,505,770	5,620,128
Other services and miscellaneous sources	22,657,958	20,324,786	42,982,744
Total Agricultural and Nonagricultural	183,234,419	173,459,970	356,694,389

According to the above table, more than two thirds of the population of India is dependent upon agricultural pursuits for livelihood, and

104

of the actual labor force also over two thirds are engaged in agriculture. But in spite of this great concentration of human effort upon the soil, India does not produce enough food for the needs of its people. Not only are vast numbers already undernourished, but the annual increase of population requires 700,000 tons of additional food grains per year. The relative inefficiency of agricultural production can be recognized in such contrasts as these: In India 75,000,000 workers till 320,000,000 acres; in the United States 8,000,000 farmers cultivate 360,000,000 acres. In India 10,000 tractors are in use; in the United States 2,500,000. In India less than 500,000 tons of fertilizer are applied to the soil in a year; in the United States 20,000,000 tons are used. The average crop yields in India are from one third to one half of those in other major agricultural countries, and of the total arable land only 16 per cent is irrigated as compared, for example, with 48 per cent in Japan.

Industry, for its part, accounts for a relatively small proportion of the wealth of India. 2,500,000 persons constitute the working force in industry, less than 2 per cent of the total laboring population. The factories account for only 7 per cent of the total national income. And foreign trade has shown a deficit every year during the past five except for 1950.

The foregoing facts outline statistically something of the colossal problem of life in India. The population is large and growing. In spite of the fact that two thirds of the people are occupied with agriculture, there is not enough food for all. Clothing, shelter, and other elementary necessities are woefully lacking.

In an attempt to face this problem, the Indian National Congress organized a National Planning Committee in 1938, and the Government of India established a new National Planning Commission in 1950. After sixteen months of work the National Planning Commission produced the draft outline of a national plan. This was made public and brought under discussion in parliament and most state legislatures, and also in meetings of representatives of industry, commerce, labor, agriculture, and other interests. After revision, the plan was presented and debated in parliament and finally adopted in December, 1952.

106

In the course of the parliamentary debates on the plan, the Communist party was completely critical. Professor Hiren Mukerjee,[1] acting leader of the Communist group, declared that the plan was most disappointing and charged the leadership which had prepared it with "betrayal of all the patriotic hopes and aspirations of the people." In his further speech he said: "We are slaves to the American Mutual Security Program. That is why our plan contemplates industrialization only to the extent that is permitted by the bigwigs of American capital, who are leading international reaction." He also added: "The food problem can only be solved by land redistribution." The Hindu Mahasabha attacked the plan somewhat less violently. Their president, N. C. Chatterjee, said that the plan had fallen on the country like a "damp squib," and had failed to galvanize the masses with

[1]*Statesman* (Calcutta), Dec. 17, 1952.

enthusiasm. There was nothing substantial in it, he declared, for the rehabilitation of the refugees, and nothing about building up war industries to make India less dependent on foreign powers for heavy armaments and war materials. The Socialist party also opposed the plan at many points, but indicated that they would cooperate in the implementation of it wherever feasible. The Planning Commission itself considers that all available knowledge and wisdom were brought to bear on the formulation of the plan, and that it is a great forward step toward the realization of the ideal of the Indian constitution to evolve a social order "in which justice, social, economic and political, shall inform all the institutions of the national life." Mr. Nehru, presenting the plan to the House of the People, stated that India was the first democratic country to adopt the idea of planning its manifold national activities, and described the goal of the planners as not merely to produce more wealth but to put an end to class inequalities and ultimately to reach a classless society. "We are trying to catch up," he said, "as far as we can, with the industrial revolution which came long years ago in Western countries and made great changes in the course of a century or more and ultimately branched off in two directions from the same tree, the two directions at present represented by the United States of America and the Soviet Union." As he thought of what the plan meant for the future, he envisioned "the mighty scene of a nation building itself, remaking itself, as all of us work together to make a new India."[2]

As adopted, the Five Year Plan proposes an expenditure of 2,069 crores[3] of rupees, or more than four hundred billion dollars. Since expenditures under the plan actually began on April 1 (the beginning of the Indian fiscal year), 1951, the five-year period will run through March, 1956. During the first two years, about 30 per cent of the contemplated total for the five years was actually expended. Of the total proposed expenditure of 20,690,000,000 rupees it is estimated that 12,580,000,000 rupees will come from the normal budgetary resources of the central and state governments. The balance will have to be covered by external assistance, additional taxation, and "deficit financing." As far as external assistance is concerned, an

[2]*Statesman* (Calcutta), Dec. 16, 1952.
[3]1 crore = 10,000,000.

108

amount equivalent to 1,560,000,000 rupees has already been obtained from abroad. The International Bank is contributing $109,800,000 in five loans. The United States of America has provided $290,000,-000. The contributions of the United States include $99,400,000 in direct grants under the Technical Assistance Agreement, and $190,-600,000 in food loans, from which the rupee proceeds were used for development. The Commonwealth countries have provided technical assistance and outright grants in lesser amounts. Soviet Russia and the People's Government of China have contributed nothing. Relative

to the possibility of increased taxation within India, it may be noted that Indian taxation now represents 7 per cent of the national income as compared with 23 per cent in the United States and 35 per cent in the United Kingdom.

Of the total expenditure under the Five Year Plan, 27 per cent is marked for development of irrigation and power, 24 per cent for transport and communications, 17 per cent for agriculture and community development, 16 per cent for social services, 8 per cent for industry, and the balance for rehabilitation and miscellaneous services. Taking irrigation and agriculture together, it is evident that a comparatively large part of the plan is directed toward the fundamental problem of increase of food production. The program in this field will utilize the services of agricultural extension workers and will emphasize the introduction of better seeds and better tools, the use of fertilizer, and the amplification of projects in reclamation and irrigation. It is estimated that by the proper use of fertilizers Indian crop yields can be increased from 30 to 100 per cent and, by provision of regular water, gains of 50 and 60 per cent can be achieved. There are already 135 river valley projects under way, and as many more in the planning stage. If all are completed, 40 or 45,000,000 acres will be added to the area under irrigation. Of these, the $150,000,000 Damodar Valley Project, for which the International Bank has made large loans, is the best known. It, alone, has been called more important to India than the Tennessee Valley Authority to the United States of America.

Further stated aims of the plan in agriculture are the reduction of disparities in wealth and income, the elimination of exploitation, the provision of security for tenant and worker, and the achievement of equality of status and opportunity for different sections of the rural population. The old zamindari system where the land was held by landlords whose rental and interest charges were so high that many peasants were in perpetual bondage, is in the process of abolition in the various states. In Orissa, for example, the government began abolition of zamindari on November 27, 1952, when 351 estates, including one which belonged to the Maharaja of Burdwan, were vested in the state government under the Orissa Estates

Abolition Act. Since the process is being conducted, however, by legal means and with reimbursement of former owners, it is slow. Meanwhile the Five Year Plan proposes an upper limit to the amount of land an individual may hold, suggests rentals not to exceed one-fourth or one-fifth of the produce, and encourages the formation of cooperative farming societies in the villages.

On October 2, 1952, the anniversary of Gandhi's birthday, fifty-five community-development projects were launched. The anticipated cost is $80,000,000, $72,000,000 to come from the Indian government, $8,000,000 from the United States of America. Each project includes approximately 300 villages with an inclusive population of some 200,000. All together 16,500 villages will be comprised in the program, with a population of 11,000,000 persons. In these areas there will be programs of improvement in sanitation, health, and education, as well as agriculture. Then these villages will become models from which the program will spread to neighboring regions.

Turning to industry, the 8 per cent allocation of Five Year Plan expenditures for this field may seem very small. Many of the irrigation projects include power developments, however, and thus the large percentage designated for irrigation and power is significant for industry as well as agriculture. Furthermore, it is considered that India has a "mixed" economy and, particularly in the program of industrial development, it is held that there is a place for a "private sector" as well as a "public sector." Thus it is anticipated that in addition to what is done through the Five Year Plan, there will be major contributions to industrial development from private sources. Considerable thought is also being given to the encouragement of small-scale industries. It is believed that a network of such enterprises, organized according to an over-all plan for production and distribution, making many things from soap to shoes, can be an important part of the entire industrial picture. By establishing these plants in the neighborhood of the villages, it is hoped to avoid many of the evils which come with the concentration of large numbers of workers in gargantuan factory cities. Even many followers of Gandhi say that such industrialization would be in harmony with the views of the great leader since he was not opposed to the use of machinery as such, but only to the centralization of industry in great cities.

In public health, India's greatest single problem is that of malaria. It is estimated that about 100 million persons suffer from it every year, and the death rate is about five per thousand inhabitants, approximately three times the rate for plague, smallpox, and cholera combined. In recognition of the magnitude of this problem, the Five Year Plan assigns top priority in health measures to malaria control, and proposes large expenditures for antimalaria drug treatments and for spraying measures in rural areas. Next to malaria, tuberculosis probably kills more people than any other disease in India, the annual mortality being said to be 500,000 at the present. The plan makes various provisions for sanatoria, hospitals, and clinics, and for vaccination with "BCG."

As a part of the health program of the Five Year Plan, a sum of 65 lakhs[1] of rupees, or about $1,300,000 has been allocated for work in family planning. The text of the plan at this point recognizes that the rapid increase in population and the pressure on the limited resources available have brought to the forefront the urgency of family planning problems. Recognizing that in the past there has been no extensive application of family planning, it is felt that the main appeal for such a procedure rests upon considerations of the health and welfare of the family. Family limitation or the spacing of children is declared to be necessary and desirable in order to secure better health for the mother and better care and upbringing for the children. Measures directed to this end should therefore, it is asserted, form a part of the public health program. Progress in this field, it is agreed, will depend first upon creating a sufficiently strong incentive in favor of family planning in the minds of the public and, next, upon providing the necessary advice and service based on acceptable, efficient, harmless and economic methods. But these presuppose intensive studies about the attitudes and motives affecting family size and techniques and procedures for the education of the public on family planning, and also field experiments on

[1] 1 lakh = 100,000.

different methods of family planning as well as medical and technical research. The program should therefore obtain an accurate picture of the factors contributing to the rapid population increase in India; discover suitable techniques of family planning and devise methods by which knowledge of these techniques can be widely disseminated; and make advice on family planning an integral part of the service of government hospitals and public health agencies. The increased interest in India in such measures as these may also be attested by the fact that the Third International Conference on Planned Parenthood was held in Bombay in November, 1952, was inaugurated by an address by Dr. S. Radhakrishnan, and received messages of greeting from Prime Minister Nehru and a number of other high officials of the Indian government. In addition, it has often been noted that as the standard of living of a country rises, the birth rate is apt to decrease and the population tends to stabilize itself.

In order to expedite all the programs of the Five Year Plan it is obviously necessary that there be an increase in literacy and education. With an 82 per cent illiteracy in India there are great obstacles in the way of the spreading of the most elementary information. Nearly half of the allotment for social services and 7 per cent of the total expenditures of the Five Year Plan is therefore designated for education. The long-range aim is to make education free and compulsory for all children between the ages of six and fourteen, a goal which will require 2,000,000 teachers and thousands of new schools. Within the scope of the present plan it is expected to increase the number of primary schools by about 20 per cent, with a consequent increase in the number of pupils in the age group of 6-11 from 44.5 per cent to 55.7 per cent. Secondary schools are estimated to increase by 18 per cent and the number of pupils by 32 per cent. At present, India has 28 universities, 40 teachers' colleges, 74 women's colleges, and more than 400 other colleges. It is expected to increase the number of these and to improve their standards. In particular it is desired to enlarge the scope of technical and vocational education, and the plan contemplates a 57 per cent increase in these institutions and a 63 per cent increase in the number of persons they train every year.

Such are some of the main outlines of the present Five Year Plan. Its proponents maintain that the plan not only will meet the most urgent needs of the national economy at the present, but also will prepare the way for a series of further plans which in twenty-seven years, according to their calculations, will double India's per capita income. The authors of the plan declare also that while in the initial stages the accent must be on increased production, even now planning should not be confined to stimulating economic activity within the existing social and economic framework of Indian life, but should aim at remolding that framework itself so as to secure progressively for all members of the community full employment, education, security against sickness and other disabilities, and adequate income. Since there is clearly a long distance to go between the present situation and the attainment of these goals, Mr. Nehru and other leaders constantly emphasize the need for every person to work and to work hard at the task which lies ahead.

Although both the Indian constitution and the Five Year Plan look toward land reform, many people in India feel that progress in this direction is being made altogether too slowly, and the Communists use this as a very strong point in their propaganda. Two or three years ago, therefore, Acharya Vinoba Bhave, a man whom many regard as the spiritual heir of Gandhi, inaugurated the Bhoodan Yagna movement as a voluntary program for "the sacrificial giving of land." Walking across the countryside like Gandhi himself, Bhave has carried his appeal directly to the people. Estimating that there are 50,000,000 people or 10,000,000 families in India who are without land, he asks all landowners both rich and poor to give one sixth of their land to those who have none. Aiming at a goal of 50,000,000 acres to be given away by 1957, he calculates that this would provide every landless family with five acres of land, an amount considered an average family holding in India. Thus far Bhave has actually secured gifts of land to the total of 1,900,000 acres. Regarded favorably by the Indian National Congress, Bhave is also strongly supported by the Socialists. Despite the age and ill health which will presumably keep him from rising to a position of

114

political leadership in any official capacity, Bhave is thus exercising a powerful influence at a significant point.

We turn now to another approach to reform of the Indian social structure, namely, the measures embodied in the Hindu Code Bill. This bill has to do in particular with the unification and modernization of the laws on marriage, divorce, inheritance, and property rights. The original Hindu Code Bill was sponsored by Dr. Ambedkar as Law Minister, and introduced in parliament in 1946 and 1947. It was an issue in the general election in 1951-1952, and was supported by Nehru. In general the most active support of the Hindu Code Bill has come from women's organizations, while opposition has come from the side of orthodox Hinduism and particularly from the right-wing political parties, the Hindu Mahasabha, the Jan Sangh, and the Ram Rajya Parishad.

In its draft form the Hindu Code Bill explained that the designation "Hindu" included all who belonged to the religions of Hinduism, Buddhism, Sikhism, and Jainism, and stated that the object of the proposed legislation was to evolve a uniform code which would apply to all the believers in these religions and would blend the most progressive elements in the various schools of law which prevail in different parts of the country. The code set forth new laws on the inheritance of property, the general effect of which would be to give women, for the first time, the same rights as men. In relation to marriage and divorce, it contained provisions which would put an end to polygamy and extend to women as well as men the rights of divorce and remarriage. It recognized both sacramental and civil marriage, and called for raising the minimum age at which girls may marry. In sacramental marriage the provision was that if the bride had not completed her sixteenth year, the consent of the guardian would be necessary; in civil marriage, that the man would have to have completed his eighteenth year, the woman her fourteenth year. It was provided that the woman might live separately and not forfeit maintenance if the husband kept a concubine in the house, was guilty of cruelty or desertion, or ceased to be a Hindu by conversion to another religion. Marriage might be dissolved in case of insanity or leprosy, desertion for more than seven years, ceasing to be a Hindu, concubinage, or prostitution. New laws were also set forth on guardianship and adoption.

Because of the opposition of certain groups to the Hindu Code Bill as a whole, it has been the recent strategy of the government to attempt to secure passage for some of its provisions in the form of separate bills. In July, 1954, it was reported that both houses of parliament had approved a bill on marriage and divorce in which monogamy is made the only lawful kind of marriage for Hindus, and divorce is allowed under certain conditions.

Finally, as we consider both the status of democracy and the attempts to solve demographic, economic, and social problems in India, we must raise the question of fundamental philosophy. Is the set of ideas which underlies Indian life conducive to the growth of democracy and capable of inspiring a sustained attack upon the problems of the social order? When we remember how complex and varied Indian philosophy is, we realize that no simple answer is possible. Nevertheless, certain observations can be made. In Hinduism, Jainism, and Buddhism, the chief native religions of India, the idea of Karma is very deep-rooted. According to this doctrine, one's status in the present life has already been determined by the deeds done in previous existences. The sum total of what one has done is one's karma; accumulated through many reincarnations, it cannot now be escaped or avoided but must be accepted. The fact that such a large segment of the human race believes in this idea suggests that there must be some measure of validity in it. It is certainly true that what is done in life affects what one is able to do in the future, and the Christian religion also speaks of how men's works follow after them. But the coupling of this truth in India with the belief in transmigration and reincarnation of souls has resulted in the conclusion that one's present state in life has to be accepted and cannot be changed. The only hope is that in a future reincarnation one will be born into a better condition. Islam, which has the most followers of any of the religions which came into India from the outside, repudiates the Hindu idea of metempsychosis but has a strong doctrine of fatalism. Allah is all-powerful, and what is and what happens are what Allah wills. The net result is similar to that of the other

116

doctrine just discussed. In both cases man must accept what is. In fact, the practical consequences of these teachings very often h[as] been of exactly this sort. Low-caste villagers have taken their [lot] with resignation; women have accepted their misfortunes as th[e] necessary fate. It would seem, therefore, that if democracy is real[l]y to grow in India, with its ideas of individual liberty and opportunity, and if the immemorial and enormous problems of economy and society are to be effectively assaulted, these age-old conceptions of an inescapable determinism must be greatly modified. Indeed there are at least some signs that this is taking place. On one occasion Mr. Nehru was asked whether determinism or fatalism was consistent with democracy. After expressing his belief that there was room for a blend of determinism and free will in Indian philosophy, he remarked that at this time what was really more important than *determinism* was the *determination* of the Indian people to consolidate their independence and protect their freedom.

The other widespread and deep-lying idea in Indian life which appears inconsonant with democracy and an obstacle in the way of social change is that of caste. There is surely a fundamental contradiction between the professed aim of the new Indian constitution to secure to all citizens "equality of status and opportunity," and the fact that the sweeper boy who will come into my room in a few minutes as I write these words, to clean the floor can never in his whole life be anything but a sweeper, no matter how bright his eyes and alert his mind, just because he was born into that caste. Untouchability, of course, is outlawed by the constitution, but the reported recent statement of the Indian representative in the United Nations, Mr. A. D. Mani, that there is no untouchability in India because the constitution has made it illegal, must be regarded as naive, to say the least. Likewise, when the prime minister was reported as making a similar statement, Dr. Ambedkar burst out, "He must be laboring under an illusion and should remedy that quickly." I myself have had cases reported to me of violent antipathy to untouchables, and have had settlements pointed out to me with perfect casualness with such words as, "That is a village of untouchables." If India is to progress to real democracy and social justice, therefore, it would seem that the evils of the caste system must certainly be eradicated although it may be that there are preservable values in it at the same time, as where one sees a son happily learning a trade in which his father is skilled.

In addition to the two major items of determinism and caste which must surely be greatly modified if India is to make the progress it desires, the Indian philosophy of religion contains miscellaneous other elements which are impediments upon the way. Many taboos, inherited rituals, and rigid beliefs hinder the application of modern and scientific methods for the improvement of the conditions of life. The almost incredible Hindu veneration of the cow makes it impossible for that animal to be scientifically bred, used for food, or killed when old or crippled, and thus India's chief beast of burden and potential source of animal food is of far less value to the country than might otherwise be. In medicine there is still excessive attachment to ancient Vedic formulas, and the prejudice against treatment of women by male physicians persists strongly. In weddings and religious festivals there is often an extravagance of expenditure which seems out of all proportion to other standards and is almost ruinous economically. Other such examples might be given but these will suffice to suggest the concrete difficulties of which there are so many in India in the way of social advance. Nevertheless, the facts cited in the last chapter and this one show that India is now definitely trying to move in the direction of its best conception of democratic life and toward a society rid of many ancient abuses.

118

9 Position

in World Affairs

What is the position of India in world affairs and its relation to the other nations? The attaining of freedom and the subsequent transition from status as a dominion to that of sovereign republic of course meant that the link of India to Great Britain was weakened, but it was not wholly severed. By action taken in 1949 India, although independent, chose to remain a member of the British Commonwealth of Nations, and thus the rights and privileges of Indians under British law were preserved. As a matter of fact, although I did not discover anyone in India who expressed a wish to be back under British rule, I did find some who spoke with a certain nostalgia of British days and who pointed out evidences of decline and disintegration since then. A rather notable example was provided at the end of 1952 by the chief justice of the Calcutta High Court, Mr. P. B. Chakravartti, when he described as "primitive institutions" the village courts then being established, and said: "The setting up of gram panchayats and panchayat committees will destroy the magnificent legal system which the British created in this country and which was chiefly responsible for the confidence of the people in the judiciary." Anyone who recalls how the Independence pledge of 1930 declared that the British government had "ruined India economically, politically, culturally, and spiritually," can scarcely help being surprised at the cordiality and affection which seem manifested almost universally in India toward Britain and the British people. The vice-president of India, Dr. S. Radhakrishnan, explained it to a friend of mine by referring to the "magnanimous gesture" with which Britain gave India its freedom and thereby wiped out all the past.

As far as earlier history is concerned, in World War I India participated with a loyalty which, in the words of Dr. Kalikinkar Datta, "won her the gratitude of Britain and the admiration of the world." More than 800,000 Indian combatants were enlisted as volunteers and served with bravery in Europe, Africa, and Western Asia. In 1917 Gandhi himself supported the appeal for soldiers and walked, in his typical way, from village to village recruiting men for the Indian army. Quantities of materials important for the war effort also came from India. In World War II the situation was different. When Britain declared war on Germany in 1939, India was automatically put into the conflict without any consultation of Indian opinion. The Indian princes supported the war, desired materials were forthcoming, and Indian recruits fought abroad. The Indian National Congress, however, and Mahatama Gandhi in particular, objected to the fact that India had been involved in the war without her own consent. In expression of disapproval, individual civil disobedience was started in 1940, and in 1942 a mass campaign of the same sort was planned. Since, at that time, there appeared to be grave danger that Germany and Japan would win the war, there was a great deal of unfavorable reaction in the West to this obstruction of the war effort by the leaders of the Indian independence movement. The response of the British government was to arrest Gandhi and many of the Congress party and thus maintain control of the situation, at least as far as possible.

At the same time, an even more outright threat was raised. A Bengali leader named Subhas Chandra Bose escaped from India, established contact with Germany and Japan, organized Indian soldiers on the Malay Peninsula into an Indian National Army with himself as Netaji or Leader, started a Government of Free India at Singapore, and in 1943 marched with the Japanese army against India. Although Bose's army surrendered after the fall of Japan, there was no little enthusiasm throughout India for this leader who, in the popular mind, assumed almost legendary proportions. His death was reported, yet it continued to be rumored that he was actually living in a foreign country. In January, 1953, there was a motion in the Corporation of Calcutta to ask the government of India to make a "searching inquiry" in China, Russia, and elsewhere, to find out if Bose were still alive and, if it were established that he was dead, to endeavor to bring back his ashes for enshrinement in India as a fitting memorial to a great national leader. On the twenty-third of the same month the fifty-seventh birthday of the hero was celebrated in West Bengal as an official holiday with elaborate ceremonies. In February it was reported that Bose's ashes were in a temple in Tokyo, and a Japanese Buddhist priest was said to be en route to India to ask Mr. Nehru to have them brought to India in a suitable manner.

It must be concluded, therefore, that while the traditional loyalty of India is to Great Britain, this alignment could again be altered by force of circumstances as it has been upon occasion in the past.

The attitude of India toward the United States of America seems to vary from appreciation and liking to criticism, suspicion, and opposition. To this observer, at any rate, there seemed to be much more friendliness toward Great Britain than toward the United States. In her book on *India and the Awakening East,* Eleanor Roosevelt expresses the opinion that the resentment previously felt toward the British was, after their departure, in large measure transferred to the United States.

The fact that, in gaining independence from British rule India was doing in the twentieth century what the United States of America had done in the eighteenth, constitutes a link between these two countries. The sympathies of the American people were doubtless almost wholly with the Indian people in their struggle which led to freedom. Although it was obviously necessary for the United States to avoid direct involvement at that time in British-Indian relations, in 1942 former President Roosevelt sent a cable to Prime Minister Churchill in which he proposed the institution of an Indian Dominion government which should last until after the end of the war. He also urged that Britain take the initiative toward the establishment of self-government in India in such a way that it would be felt the offer was made cheerfully and willingly. Harry Hopkins said that probably no other suggestion from the same source was received so wrathfully by Mr. Churchill. Afterward, Colonel Louis Johnson came to India to participate unofficially and as the American president's personal representative in British-Indian negotiations. Such facts as these were recognized by those who were aware of them as indicating the interest of the United States in the Indian national cause. In 1946 the United States repealed the legislation which had previously made permanent immigration or naturalization impossible for Indians, and passed a law by which they were eligible for citizenship. This act was greeted as at least a rectification, welcome if tardy, of a long-standing and unfavorable discrimination. In recent times the gifts of food and loans of money which have come to India from the United States have been received with some appreciation. It is also reported that in the five years prior to 1950 approximately 6,000 Indian students studied in the United States. From frequent personal observation I can state that the fine library of the United States Information Service in Calcutta is constantly crowded with Indians reading American books and magazines. A Hindu friend told me, however, that probably 80 per cent of the students utilizing these resources are Communists. In addition, it may be recalled that when Mr. Nehru visited the United States in 1949 and spoke at the University of California in Berkeley, he said: "The picture of the average American presented to the outside world is a hard-headed, efficient and practical business man, intent on making money and using that money to add to his power and influence. That picture, no doubt, has some truth in it. And yet there is another picture, and, I think, a much more enduring one, of a warm-hearted and very generous people, full of goodwill to others and with a firm belief in the basic principles on which this great republic was founded—the principles of freedom, equality and democracy. It has been my good fortune to see this picture wherever I have gone and this has made me realize

122

wherein lies the real strength of America. Everywhere I have found a love of freedom and a desire for peace and cooperation, and, among the people, a frankness and human approach which make a friendly understanding easy."

Criticism by India of life in the United States focuses largely upon two issues. The first is that of racial injustice. Despite the fact that there is very real color prejudice in India, many of the lighter-skinned looking down upon the darker-skinned, it seems universally to be believed that the United States is the prime exponent of discrimination against people of color. The willingness of many Americans to confess our truly lamentable failures in this regard, the desire of many to work for amelioration of the situation, and the existence of many improvements already accomplished, seem to count for little over against the indubitable facts of the injustice which has been practiced and that which still remains. Questions on the racial problem in the United States are almost always those which are put first and most insistently to American speakers in India, although at the same time the questioners seem to assume that they are already in full possession of all the facts and are indisposed to alter their opinions of the situation no matter what is said to them. More attention is paid, however, when the speaker is himself a Negro. A good example was provided by Dr. Benjamin Mays, president of Morehouse College, Atlanta, Georgia, on his recent visit to Lucknow. This distinguished educator said among other things: "Of course the problem in the United States has not been solved, but it is getting better. There are about a dozen Negro judges in America. Many of our top educationists are Negroes. There are several Negroes in the state legislatures. Some of our leading preachers and ministers of religion are Negroes. Some of the leading lawyers are Negroes. Most of the movements that have brought about the improvements have been initiated by Negroes themselves with considerable support from the liberal white people of America." These and other words of his were quoted at length in the press and given prominent publicity.

The second issue which is brought up repeatedly and critically is that of the supposed "materialism" of the United States of America. It is widely held that American culture is thoroughly materialistic,

123

quite lacking in spiritual elements, and this in contrast with India which is supposed to be a true home of things of the spirit. Aside from the amount of misinterpretation involved in such a contrast, there is also a latent contradiction between this violent criticism and the strong desire for material assistance from the United States. The often unrecognized inconsistency in the Indian attitude was aptly pointed out by George E. Jones when he remarked that "they admire our material advancement and suspect our materialism."

Suspicion is also directed against the United States when it proffers economic assistance and when capital investments in India are under consideration. Although it is often felt that the United States does too little to aid India, what is done is viewed often with apprehension. Having been so long under foreign domination politically, there is real fear lest India pass now under foreign domination economically. There is alarm about what J. J. Singh called "a new imperialism of dollar penetration." So help is wanted, yet help is resisted. When Dr. Henry F. Grady was ambassador to India he observed the same contradiction. On one occasion he remarked publicly that if a country is afraid of "domination" by foreign capital it is certainly justified in passing laws which will keep capital out; but it is decidedly inconsistent if, at the same time, the leaders of the country complain that capital does not come in. Grady went on to declare strongly that there was no basis for the contention of "certain unfriendly writers," or the suspicion of "others who would like to be our friends," that the United States of America is in any wise trying to gain control over other nations when it extends assistance to them. These affirmations of the former ambassador still seem pertinent.

Opposition to the United States appears at numerous points. In the economic realm, insofar as the American system is one of "free enterprise," Indian thinking goes against it. At least as far as applicability to India is concerned, it appears that most Indians would attack "free enterprise" and would defend some kind of socialistic state. In international affairs, there is great fear of war, and American policies are always combated when it is thought that they will increase the likelihood or scope of armed conflict. The

124

Southeast Asia Treaty Organization, formed by several nations including the United States of America in the summer of 1954, was opposed by Mr. Nehru on the ground that it would "only increase international tension." Most grievous of all, no doubt, in the eyes of India at this time is the fact that the United States has made a military assistance pact with Pakistan. The point at which this impinges most heavily and most unfavorably upon India is with regard to Kashmir. India and Pakistan advance rival claims for Kashmir. In the conflict a truce was made and mediation sought through the United Nations. Now, when a settlement has not yet been achieved, to have arms supplied by the United States to Pakistan seems to give a fresh advantage to Pakistan and to do harm to the interests of India.

All in all, then, it must be concluded that there are important links of sympathy and mutuality between India and the United States of America, but that there are also large areas of disagreement and that any automatic alignment between the two countries is by no means to be assumed.

In regard to China the prevailing Indian attitude seems to be one of friendliness and hopefulness; it is natural that India should desire to maintain good relations with its nearest large neighbor. The Communist revolution in China is regarded as fundamentally a movement of Chinese nationalism. It is argued that China was driven to its present orientation toward and dependence upon the Union of Soviet Socialist Republics by the actions of the United States in aiding Chiang Kai-shek at the close of World War II and afterward giving him the protection of the American fleet, and of the United Nations in sending forces across the thirty-eighth parallel in Korea and thereby threatening the Chinese mainland, and in refusing Communist China a place in the United Nations. When South Korea was invaded in 1950 and the United Nations named North Korea as the aggressor, India supported the move; but when in 1951 the United Nations decided that Communist China was guilty of aggression in Korea, India joined with the members of the Russian-dominated group in voting against the resolution. India steadily maintains that Communist China should be admitted to the United Nations, and that that body is incomplete and untrue to its name without the presence of China. Thus Mr. Nehru was quoted in December, 1952, as saying: "The Government of India have always felt strongly in favor of admission of the People's Government of China into the United Nations. In fact, it has been our belief that no problem in the Far East can be solved without the concurrence of the Government of China and without their coming into the United Nations." For the future, India hopes that, when the Chinese People's Government becomes firmly established, the country will pursue its own independent course and will not be subordinate to Russia or any foreign power. Then India and China can stand together as the friends they have always desired to be, and as partners in Asian affairs. Returning from a visit to China in November, 1954, Nehru declared that such friendship between India and China is "essential for the peace and progress of Asia."

In relation to Russia, India seems guardedly admiring. With their Gandhian heritage of belief in nonviolence, many Indians cannot approve the more obvious displays of Soviet force and ruthlessness either abroad or at home. But in their own struggle for economic betterment, a great many of the people of India seem to feel some sense of kinship with the people of Russia. Upon the occasion of his visit to Moscow, Nehru was impressed, as we have seen, by the spirit he sensed among the common people and by their determination to achieve a new life for themselves. We have already quoted Nehru in his statement that the Soviet Union and the United States of America represent the two directions in which the industrial revolution has branched off, that revolution with which India is now trying to catch up; and it seems evident that the Five Year Plan in connection with which he made this remark, owes not only its name but much of its entire inspiration to the Russian example. It is also often pointed out that Russia shows how a country can modernize and industrialize itself without coming under obligation to foreign capital, and thus it is felt that guidance can be found there for what India is now undertaking for herself. In spite of many violent actions such as the recent anti-Jewish purge, Russia is also looked upon as a land where the

126

hated racial discrimination believed characteristic of the United States does not exist.

In the present state of world affairs, then, India has leanings toward both the Western democracies and the Eastern totalitarianisms. As far as the words are concerned, India would claim loyalty to the ideals of democracy and disclaim belief in totalitarianism. As far as the substance of the matter is concerned, she is critical of much which the United States and other Western powers call democracy and sympathetic to much which is found in Russia and China. Actually and by her own statement, it is the intention of India to stand neither with the Western democracies nor with the opposing Eastern powers. This has been called an "in-between" policy, or a policy of "aloofness from power blocs." As early as 1948 Nehru observed that the world was split into two power blocs, and declared that India would take care not to side with one group or another for temporary gains. He said that India wanted to be friendly with every country but to follow its own policy on every question and to remain neutral on matters by which it was not directly affected. In December, 1952,[1] he was quoted in public address as saying: "Whether there is a cold war or a shooting war India will keep aloof. India will guard the peace as long as she can, but when the shooting begins she will not be involved. This is the basis of our foreign policy and nobody can stampede us into doing anything else." And in January, 1953, the Working Committee of the Indian National Congress adopted this resolution: "The Congress records its appreciation of and support to the Government of India in pursuing steadfastly, unhindered by setbacks, inducements and provocations, the policy of peace and international cooperation, and non-alignment with power blocs, and urges the Government to continue to pursue this course which alone enables it to make a positive contribution towards international understanding and world peace."

While the stated policy thus enunciates a desire to stay aloof from power blocs, it also appears to be aimed at the formation of what would actually be a third bloc of states on the international scene, a grouping of Asian and perhaps Arab powers which would be aligned with

[1]*Statesman*, Dec. 7, 1952

the leadership neither of Russia nor of the United States but would, it is hoped, be a stabilizing force between the two. If China were ultimately to stand with such a group it is believed it would have much weight. It was therefore of no little interest when India recently joined with the other so-called Colombo powers, Pakistan, Burma, Ceylon, and Indonesia, in issuing a call for a conference of thirty states of Asia and Africa to meet in April, 1955. Included in the invitation is Communist China as well as many but not all of the other governments in the Far East, the Middle East, and Africa. The outcome of the meeting will deserve careful attention.

An earlier example of the attempted implementation of the Indian policy in international affairs could be seen in the draft proposal for peace in Korea which India placed before the General Assembly of the United Nations in November-December, 1952. The outcome also illustrates the difficulties India must expect in trying to carry through such a position. The United States responded unfavorably to the plan at first, but then came to support it as did fifty-four countries all together. The Soviet bloc of five nations voted against the proposal, and the Soviet Foreign Minister Andrei Vishinsky attacked the chief architect of the Indian plan, V. K. Krishna Menon, with the words, "You by your resolution are trying to push people into the holocaust of war." In regard to a statement by Mr. Menon that India speaks for the Asians from the Middle East to the Pacific Ocean, Vishinsky also declared: "We understand the position of the Chinese peoples and refuse to recognize the right of anyone to speak on behalf of the Asians." This episode seemed to show that China was, in fact, a puppet of the Soviet power, and if that was the case, then one of the main postulates of the Indian foreign policy was revealed as an illusion.

When the truce was established in Korea, the United Nations turned to India for the chairmanship of the Repatriation Commission, and Indian troops were sent to Korea to supervise the exchange of prisoners of war. Relative to the assumption of this responsibility, an American observer in India commented on the tact that would be required if India were to please, at one and the same time, the United Nations, the United States, the U.S.S.R., Communist China and Dr. Syng-

128

man Rhee. At the end of September, 1953, a riot was reported from Panmunjom in which thousands of anti-Communist Chinese prisoners clashed with Indian troops, and in which the ability of the Indians to deal with a difficult situation was remarkably revealed. In protest against the release of one of their number to the Communists, the other prisoners stoned Indian guards and dragged two Indian officers into their compound. The commanding general of the Indian troops, Major General S. P. P. Thorat, proceeded into the compound with twelve men. The frenzied Chinese, armed with tent poles, attacked Thorat's men who had only sticks as weapons. Chinese and North Korean prisoners in other enclosures started to demonstrate and it appeared they might storm the barbed-wire fences and overrun all the Indian troops. But Thorat put down the riot with what was described as a magnificent psychological move. "What sort of Chinese are you?" he said to the nearest Chinese. "Where is your hospitality? You have offered my men neither tea nor cigarettes." The Chinese were stunned, their anger melted away, they dropped their weapons— and brought out tea and cigarettes. After polite discussion the two hostages were released, and Thorat and his men were escorted to the gate by a guard of honor in admiration of their bravery.

During the time that war was going on in Indochina, it was the almost universal opinion in India that France should give independence to the associated states of Indochina immediately. To the question whether the withdrawal of France would not open the way for complete Communist domination in that area and thereby provide a threat to India itself, the answer was commonly given that the establishment of a nation's independence is the only effective way in which to combat Communism within it. Nevertheless, if Communist forces active not only in Indochina but also in Malaya and Burma should continue to be successful, it cannot be doubted that there would be great danger to India.

At the present, it is on the Tibetan border that India has come into immediate confrontation with Communist power. In 1950 Chinese troops were sent into Tibet to "liberate Tibetan people and defend the frontier of China." In 1951 a Chinese-Tibetan agreement was signed under which Peking promised to respect the autonomy of

Tibet, preserve its political system, and guarantee its religious freedom. At the same time, however, it was provided that the Dalai Lama should share authority with the Panchen Lama, who is pro-Chinese, that the foreign relations of Tibet should be determined by China, and the Tibetan forces be integrated with the Chinese army. Thus for all practical purposes Tibet was brought completely under Chinese Communist control. Since India has traditionally supported the autonomy of Tibet, in 1950 New Delhi protested to Peking that "the invasion by Chinese troops in Tibet cannot but be regarded as deplorable and in the considered judgment of the Indian government, not in the interest of China or of peace." In 1951, however, Nehru told the Indian parliament: "We were aggrieved at a certain turn of events in Tibet, but we did not allow that to affect our policy or our

130

desire to maintain friendly relations with the People's Government of China." And in 1952 India acquiesced in a Chinese demand that the Indian Mission in Lhasa be withdrawn and a Consulate General established there accredited directly to China and not to Tibet. This action was equivalent to recognition that no vestige of Tibetan independence remained.

From Tibet, Communist pressure can be increasingly applied all along India's northern frontier. The Himalayas are no longer adequate guarantee against attack. It is known that a road for motor transport is being built on the ancient caravan route which comes over high passes from Lhasa and enters India at Kalimpong. In February, 1953, it was reported that 4,000 Chinese troops were in the Chumbi valley on the Tibetan side of the frontier, turning the area into a military stronghold, and Indian merchants trading there were prohibited from taking any photographs. In July, 1953, M. P. Koirala, the premier of Nepal, said he had definite information that Chinese Communist forces occupying Tibet had built an airport near the northeastern boundary of Nepal and another near the northwestern frontier. The latter would be within 300 miles of New Delhi. In Nepal, Sikkim, Bhutan, and Darjeeling, Communist activity has been growing, and it was reported in 1953 that the Chinese had printed a map of China in which Bhutan and Sikkim are shown as part of China or Tibet. In the northwest, passes like the famous Khyber have from time immemorial been avenues of invasion of India. If a hostile move came from that direction it would affect Pakistan first; in spite of that, the inclusion of Pakistan in British and American defense strategy in the Middle East has been denounced by Probodh Chander, chief parliamentary secretary from the Indian Punjab, as an act of unfriendliness to India inasmuch as it might invite aggression from Russia. And Mr. Nehru said about arms aid from the United States to Pakistan: "It is a matter of most intense concern to us. Pakistan can have bases, foreign armies, and anything it likes. It is open to it to give up its independence if it likes or limit it, but we are concerned with the consequences of these actions and watching developments with the greatest care."

It remains to be seen, then, whether India's attempt to occupy a middle position will prove a fruitful contribution, as is hoped, to world peace; or whether it will prove to be impossible to maintain a position of neutrality on the question of democracy and totalitarianism. In the meantime, it is not unimportant to have as realistic an understanding as possible of the Indian position and, on the basis of that understanding, to work in every way possible for honorable and effective cooperation between the United States of America and India in the cause of world peace.

10 Perils

of the Peaks

In all the world the highest mountains are those which form the northern boundary of the Indo-Pakistani subcontinent. These are the Himalaya, "the abode of snow," and adjacent ranges. They form a natural and spectacular frontier on the north for Pakistan, India, and the several small states normally dependent upon India, Nepal, Sikkim, and Bhutan. These mighty mountains may be seen in superlative grandeur from Kashmir, Darjeeling, and other points.

The vale of Kashmir is an oval plain, drained by the Jhelum River, a tributary of the Indus. Eighty-five miles long and twenty-five broad, the valley lies at an average elevation of 5,200 feet. It is entirely surrounded by mountains, the Himalayas curving in from the east, the Karakoram lying farther to the north, and lesser ranges standing on the west and south. At the western end of the main Himalayas and less than one hundred miles north of Srinagar is the peak of Nanga Parbat, 26,660 feet high; in the heart of the Karakoram and less than two hundred miles north and east of Srinagar is K2, also known as Mount Godwin Austen or Lamba Pahar, 28,250 feet in elevation. In the Karakoram range there are thirty-three summits higher than 24,000 feet; in the watershed of the Hunza River which

cuts through the Karakoram there are said to be more peaks over 20,000 feet in height than there are mountains over 10,000 feet in the Alps. Such is the tremendous world of rock and snow and ice, the edges of which are visible from the valley of Kashmir. In the valley itself there is much beauty too. Srinagar is interlaced by canals; the famous Dal Lake, five miles long, is covered with floating gardens and lotus flowers. Of Kashmir, Sir Francis Younghusband wrote: "The country with which one is most apt to compare it is, naturally, Switzerland. And Switzerland, indeed, has many charms and combination of lakes and mountains in which, I think, it excels Kashmir. But it is built on a smaller scale. There is not the same wide sweep of snow-clad mountains. There is no place where one can see a complete circle of snowy mountains surrounding a plain of anything like the length and breadth of the Kashmir Valley for the main valleys of Switzerland are like the side valleys of Kashmir. And above everything, there is at the back of Kashmir, and visible in glimpses from the southern side—a region of stupendous mountains surpassing every other in the world."

Darjeeling is at the extreme north of India at the eastern side. Flying northward from Calcutta, before the airplane lands at Bagdogra, Mount Everest, Makalu, and Kanchenjunga are visible almost directly ahead. From Siliguri the two-foot gauge Darjeeling Himalayan Railway and a parallel narrow road climb steeply up into the foothills.

134

Leaving the glistening, steaming plains behind, winding and twisting up mountain slopes often heavily swathed in clouds, these avenues of travel lead in somewhat over fifty miles to Darjeeling. The town is built upon a ridge over 7,000 feet high, and its shops, houses, and buildings are scattered over the mountainside in a most picturesque way. The apex of the ridge, called Observatory Hill, is crowned by a small shrine where Hindu and Buddhist deities are worshiped and where innumerable prayer flags flutter from tall bamboo poles. Often the clouds swirl around Darjeeling, magnifying its mystery and beauty. When the clouds part, Kanchenjunga is revealed, fifty miles to the north, 28,166 feet in elevation. Going out past Ghoom, where Buddhist lamas of the Yellow Sect blow their long temple horns, and up to 8,500-foot Tiger Hill, Mount Everest also comes into view again, somewhat over one hundred miles away to the northwest. The

height of Mount Everest was originally calculated at 29,002 feet; it is now commonly given as 29,141 feet; a new survey is planned by the government of India which may change the figure slightly. Not far southeast of Everest, Makalu rises to 27,790 feet.

To the people who dwelt nearest them, the mighty mountains were for long an object of superstitious dread. They were pictured as the abode of deities and the haunt of demons. Indeed, among many these beliefs still persist. Pilgrims and traders pile heaps of stones upon the passes to appease the spirits. They dread the poison which works on the high places to cause dizziness and swelling and nausea and suffocation. They tell of dragons whose breath is an icy blast and who spew out boulders to overwhelm the traveler. They describe snow snakes one hundred feet in length which pursue men who try to climb the peaks. Although emancipated from these primitive conceptions, modern man feels himself at the mercy of forces far greater than himself when he goes among the great mountains. Nor has all the mystery quite disappeared, either, as testified by those who have found in Himalayan snows the large backward footprints of a creature which they have never yet seen or identified for sure, the so-called "abominable snowman."

It was not the people who dwelt at the base of the highest peaks in the world, therefore, who first undertook to climb them. Rather it was men from the West, men driven by the same kind of impulsion which sent others from there across uncharted seas, into remote deserts, and to the Poles of earth. One of them, the British climber Mallory, who was later to lose his life on Mount Everest, was once asked why he wanted to climb the highest mountain in the world. Thinking out his answer for a moment, he replied, "Because it is there." The existence of these high peaks, often appearing to be beyond human capacity to surmount and in many cases thus far proving to be so indeed, has exerted a compelling attraction upon men whose strongest urge is to attempt what is difficult or even apparently impossible.

Nanga Parbat was the scene of the first serious effort to climb one of these giant peaks. A. F. Mummery, who had distinguished himself with almost incredible ascents in the Alps, came to Nanga Parbat in 1895. Climbing with two Gurkha porters, he was turned

136

back on his first try. Returning to his bivouac on a rock rib projecting five hundred feet from the mountainside, he found his gear had been swept away by an avalanche of ice. Crossing the glacier to make a new attempt upon the peak, he and his porters disappeared and no trace of them was ever found. The mighty mountain had shown its formidable strength, but the history of man's fight to gain the highest summits in the world had begun.

In 1932 Willi Merkl of Munich led a party of Germans and Americans to 23,000 feet on Nanga Parbat. At that point storms drove them back, and on the way home belated tragedy struck when one of the climbers, Rand Herron, fell to his death from the Second Pyramid in Egypt. In 1934 Merkl headed another strong group at Nanga Parbat. Not far above the base of the mountain, one of the men died of pneumonia. The others went on up. They reached a point which they judged to be in striking distance of the summit. A storm of incredible severity broke. Three climbers and six porters died from exposure on the way down. In 1937 Karl Wien was the leader of a new attempt. In May the party left Srinagar, crossed the Tagbal and Burzil passes, and on May 22 began their assault upon the mountain. From a base camp at 13,000 feet they established Camp I on the highest extremity of the moraine above a great glacier. Eight hours of toilsome climbing above that, at the foot of a towering ice fall, they pitched Camp II. The ice cliffs collapsed and destroyed the camp. On June 3 they launched their second attempt. Now they went higher. They succeeded in establishing Camps III and IV, the latter at 20,400 feet. Through deep snow they climbed upward, almost to the point of making Camp V at 21,780 feet, but had to return to Camp IV. During the night of June 14-15 an avalanche of terrific proportions descended upon Camp IV. An area of fifteen acres was covered with gigantic ice blocks, some the size of a house. The camp was obliterated, seven climbers and nine Sherpa porters were buried. Wien, at a lower camp, was the sole survivor. When the news reached Germany, Paul Bauer, head of the German Himalayan Foundation, and two companions came by air to India. By special arrangement they were flown up the gorge of the Indus River. Ascending to the site of Camp IV, they found an ice ax. Digging through solidly frozen ice, at eleven feet below the surface they were able to recover the bodies of five of the seven climbers and all of their diaries. Nanga Parbat's ice wall shimmered above, still impregnable.

In the summer of 1953 a German and Austrian team returned to the attack. There were ten men in the group, and the leader was Peter Aschenbrenner, a veteran of the 1934 and 1937 expeditions. They established base camp in Fairy Tale Meadow at 14,670 feet, only to be held up there for several days by heavy snowstorms. Then they pushed a series of advance camps toward the summit, until position was gained for the climactic endeavor. Finally on July 3 the Austrian Herman Buhl, known as one of the most daring climbers in Europe, pushed on toward the summit. Leaving a high camp at about 23,000 feet he proceeded by himself and without oxygen. On the top he planted the flags of the West German Republic and of Pakistan. It was already evening and he was not able to descend far before darkness forced him to halt. In spite of the bitter cold he survived the exposure of the night and in the light of the next morning completed his return to the camp where his fellows met him. The almost incredible victory came only thirty-six days after the first ascent of Everest to be described later in this chapter.

The first attempt to climb Kanchenjunga, third highest mountain in the world, was made in 1905. Already, in 1849, Joseph Hooker visited the area. In 1899 Douglas Freshfield made a circuit of the mountain and wrote *Round Kangchenjunga*; Vittorio Sella accompanied him and took superb photographs. Between 1907 and 1921 when he died on the first Everest expedition, A. M. Kellas climbed in the vicinity and was the first systematically to employ and train Sherpa and Bhutia porters. But the first real endeavor to climb the mountain was that made by Aleister Crowley of England and three companions from Switzerland in 1905. Their highest camp was at 20,343 feet; some climbed perhaps a thousand feet higher. Making a descent in steep snow, an avalanche was precipitated, and one Swiss climber and three porters buried. In 1929 E. F. Farmer of New York attempted the ascent and disappeared upon the mountain. In the same year Paul Bauer and the German Himalayan climbers with

138

great difficulty reached the crest of an ice ridge which promised a way on up. Snow began to fall every day, and for refuge they cut caves in the solid ice. Camp X was finally pitched on a snow slope at 22,288 feet. Above that they climbed to 24,272 feet, their highest point. A terrible storm deposited seven feet of snow in a single day, and they descended amidst fearsome avalanches. In 1930 a party from Germany, Austria, Switzerland, and Great Britain, including F. S. Smythe and led by G. Dyhrenfurth, went through Nepal and established their base camp on the northwest side of Kanchenjunga. They spent a week making a way up an ice wall in order to gain the north ridge of the mountain. The ice wall collapsed, masses of ice as high as cathedrals toppled down and stopped two hundred yards from their camp. Trying the northwest ridge, they ascended knife-like edges of ice and passed around great pinnacles of rock but finally had to acknowledge defeat. During nineteen days on the mountain, ice avalanches had fallen every night and day. In 1931 Bauer and the Germans returned and after incredible difficulties reached 25,700 feet. The summit was a half mile higher than that.

Siniolchum is east of Kanchenjunga, a rock-and-ice pyramid of almost perfect symmetry, 22,620 feet high. When Freshfield first saw it he called it "the most beautiful mountain in the world." Bauer and his companions passed near it in 1929 and judged it "the very embodiment of inaccessibility." In 1936 they undertook to climb it. Crossing the Zemu glacier and reaching the moraine of the Siniolchum glacier, they bivouacked at the snow line. They toiled up through snow into which they sank to the knees at each step. The next day they negotiated one ice fall, then another. On the following day they ascended an incredibly steep ice corridor and attained the ridge above. Climbing the ridge at an angle of at least 70 degrees, they slept in a yawning cleft. A steep ridge ran to the summit 1,500 feet above. One pitch, only 200 feet high, cost much time. On the ridge they crossed a more perilous and exposed spot than they had ever seen in the Alps. They passed over terraces covered with soft, powdery snow. They made an arduous traverse on solid ice coated with snow which was like flour. They stepped upon the summit, a precipitous and exposed place beneath which the deeply furrowed south ridge fell away and the incredible north precipice plunged into the depths. Afterward they wrote: "That which we seek and strive for, yet only vaguely sense and can never fully realize, seemed at that moment embodied in the purest clarity."

Kamet is a 25,447-foot peak in the Central Himalaya. Climbed in 1931, it was the first of the seventy Himalayan peaks over 25,000 feet to be ascended. In 1855 the Schlagintweit brothers made a pioneering attempt upon the mountain. In 1907 T. G. Longstaff and C. G. Bruce conducted a reconnaissance. In 1911 A. Morris Slingsby reached about 22,000 feet. In 1912-1913 C. F. Meade found the right route on the east side and got to 22,000 feet. In 1920 A. M. Kellas attained 23,600 feet. In 1931 the successful party was led by F. S. Smythe. From a base camp at 15,500 feet they pushed up the East Kamet glacier, ascended a *couloir*, gained a ridge, and came out on a pass called Meade's Col in honor of its discoverer. Establishing five advance camps all together, they were at last in position to try for the summit. From Camp V, eight and one-half hours' work was required to climb the 2,300 feet which remained to the top. The last ice slope had a steepness of over 50 degrees. Gasping for breath, the climbers labored up this slope, passed along a knifelike crest of snow, descended into a shallow gap, and came up upon two rounded domes of snow which formed the summit.

Nanda Devi is also in the Central Himalaya and at 25,649 feet is the highest peak in that region. In 1934 E. E. Shipton and H. W. Tilman pushed their way up the extremely forbidding gorge of the Rishi Ganga River and penetrated the "inner sanctuary" at the foot of Nanda Devi. In 1936 Tilman returned with a party of British and American climbers who succeeded in reaching the summit, the highest peak climbed up to that time.

Rakaposhi is in the Karakoram in the extreme northwest. Called Dumani or "Necklace of Clouds" by the Hunza people, it is 25,550 feet high. Seen and mentioned by W. M. Conway in 1892, Rakaposhi was ascended to about 20,000 feet by Campbell H. Secord and J. M. K. Vyvyan in 1938, and to about the same height by H. W. Tilman, Hans Gyr, Robert Kappeler, and Secord in 1947.

140

Annapurna, in Nepal, is 26,493 feet or 8,075 meters high. As higher and higher summits were reached, it became a sort of goal to ascend a peak of 8,000 meters elevation. That hope was realized in 1950 when a French Himalayan expedition, led by Maurice Herzog, climbed Annapurna. They had the threefold task for the first time of finding a way to reach the mountain, of making a reconnaissance to determine a practicable route to the top, and of accomplishing the ascent. It had been confidently declared that no expedition could do all three things on a single trip, but this one did. Penetrating a savage and desolate cirque of mountains never before seen by men from the West, they established base camp at the foot of a spur of the peak. They were already about as high as the summit of Mont Blanc. Annapurna loomed above them like a fortress, defended by a great barrier wall 23,000 feet high. Camp I was placed at 16,750 feet, Camp II at 19,350 feet with a "cauliflower ridge," as they called it, of ice and snow in the background. Camp III was among the sércs at 21,650 feet, Camps IV and V along the curving "sickle" which led toward the summit. Climbing the final icy *couloir* with crampon-shod feet, Herzog and his companion Lachenal stopped at every step to gasp in the insufficient air. The summit was a corniced crest of ice with terrifying precipices on the far side. Of their sentiments upon attaining the goal, they said that their hearts overflowed with unspeakable happiness. But great disasters were to befall the two men. Herzog took pictures, lost his gloves, and froze his hands; both men suffered frostbitten feet. Staggering down the mountain they were assailed by a howling storm, became lost, and had to spend the night at the bottom of a crevasse. An avalanche of powdered snow poured in upon them there, burying their boots and necessitating a long search to recover them. Farther down, part of the heavily weighted snow slope crumbled away and Herzog was precipitated into a vertical ice shaft where he hung head downward at the end of a rope. Two other members of the party, Rébuffat and Terray, finally met Herzog and Lachenal and led them on down, but themselves became blinded from the snow. Terribly frostbitten, Herzog lost all his fingers and toes, Lachenal all of his toes. In his account of the ascent in *The Himalayan Journal* for 1950-1951,

Herzog remarked that instead of Annapurna, "goddess of the harvest," the peak should have been named Kali, "the beautiful but cruel." Yet in the conclusion of the book which describes the climb, written by Herzog while still in a Paris hospital, he spoke of how he and his companions adored the mountains with the simplicity of a child, and revered them with the veneration of a monk for the divine. Looking ahead, he remarked that there are other Annapurnas in the lives of men.

The first attempt on 27,790-foot Makalu in the Mount Everest region, fifth highest peak in the world, was made in the summer of 1954 by an American Himalayan Expedition led by William Siri of the University of California at Berkeley. The party encountered very bad weather and extremely steep mountain slopes, but reached a little over 23,500 feet before being forced to turn back.

K2 was the surveyor's designation and has remained the best known name for the 28,250-foot peak which is the highest in the Karakoram and the second highest known in the world. The first attempt to climb K2 was in 1902 by O. Eckenstein; the second in 1909 by the Duke of the Abruzzi. In 1938 the American Alpine Club sent an expedition there, led by Charles S. Houston and participated in by Paul K. Petzoldt and others. Houston and Petzoldt reached about 26,000 feet upon the peak, Petzoldt going alone several hundred feet higher still and photographing himself at the highest point by tripping the shutter of his camera with his ice ax. In 1939 another American party, led by Fritz Wiessner, attained approximately 27,000 feet. One member, Dudley Wolfe, remained temporarily alone at a high camp; three porters attempted to return to him; none of the four ever came down off the mountain, and what actually happened to them still remains a mystery. A third American expedition, again under the leadership of Charles S. Houston, went to the mountain in the summer of 1953. From base camp at 16,500 feet, eight climbers struggled up the stupendous peak until Camp VIII was occupied at 25,500 feet. It was hoped that Camp IX could be pitched at 27,000 feet and the summit attempted from there, but unremitting storms of terrific intensity pinned the climbers to their Camp VIII tents for nine days. Then Arthur Gilkey, one of the men

who would have made the summit try on the first good day, suffered a blood clot in his left leg. In the attempt to save his life the party started back down while the storm was still raging. Five hundred feet down the mountainside they anchored the sick man temporarily to a hard wall of snow. A slip occurred and five climbers fell 200 feet down a 50-degree slope, but were arrested in their descent by the belay of one man above. Although all five were injured in some degree, with the assistance of the other two they were able to climb back at last to their original positions. But when they returned to where Arthur Gilkey had been, an avalanche had swept him away to presumable immediate death.

In 1954 the Italian Alpine Club sent an expedition to the mountain their fellow countryman, the Duke of the Abruzzi, had attempted so many years before. Led by Ardito Desio, the party included eleven climbers and seven scientists. They were delayed by the desertion of their porters, afflicted by the death from pneumonia of one of the climbers, Mario Puchoz, and pinned to their shelters by forty days of continual storms. Nevertheless, they pushed a series of nine camps up the Abruzzi Ridge, the highest being placed at 26,600 feet. From there in better weather on July 31 Achille Compagnoni and Lino Lacedelli started for the summit. Toiling up through deep snow, they exhausted their supplies of oxygen, but went doggedly on, gasping in the insufficient air. So slow was their progress that it was six o'clock in the evening when they stood on the top. Descending in the dark, they returned late in the night to their companions at Camp VIII, staggering and dazed from lack of oxygen, bruised from falls, and with frostbitten hands, but victorious. The second highest mountain in the world had been climbed.

The highest of all the Himalayan peaks and, unless future discovery proves otherwise, the highest mountain in the world, is Mount Everest. This mountain is almost hidden behind other ranges and its supreme height was not recognized until 1852. In that year a computer of the Trigonometrical Survey of the Indian Government, working on observations made three years before, for the first time calculated the elevation of the peak. He announced the result to his chief with the words, "Sir, I have discovered the highest mountain in the world!" The surveyor general named the peak after his own predecessor, Sir George Everest, and it has been commonly known as Mount Everest ever since. The Tibetan name, however, is Chomo Lungma, "Goddess Mother of the World."

In 1921 the first of a series of British expeditions went to Everest and reconnoitered the mountain thoroughly. In 1922 a second expedition undertook the ascent. A long circuit through Tibet brought the climbers to the Rongbuk monastery twenty miles due north of the peak. There they saw the chief lama who is considered the high priest of the sacred mountain which looms up so grandly at the head of the valley. The base camp of the expedition was established at 16,500 feet on the Rongbuk Glacier, Camps I and II were on the East Rongbuk glacier. Camp III was at the foot of the North col, Camp IV on its crest at 22,900 feet. From there George Leigh-Mallory, E. F. Norton, and T. H. Somervell tried for the top and in two days reached just under 27,000 feet. A second team, George Finch and Geoffrey Bruce, went up using oxygen and got to just over 27,000 feet. All endured bitter cold and howling gales of wind, but all returned safely. Regathering in their lower camps, they planned another attempt. New snow had fallen. Climbing to the North col, the party was caught in an avalanche and seven porters were lost.

The climbers came back in 1924. In 1922 they had only bivouacked above Camp IV, now two higher camps were placed upon the mountain: Camp V at 25,300 feet, Camp VI at 26,800 feet. E. F. Norton, accompanied the first part of the way by T. H. Somervell, traversed sloping slabs five or six hundred feet below the crest of Everest's northeast ridge, crossed a great *couloir*, and reached a point 28,126 feet high on the final pyramid of the peak. George Mallory and A. C. Irvine went up, using oxygen, preferring the very crest of the main ridge of the mountain. As Noel Odell watched from 26,000 feet, the mists cleared momentarily and he saw two tiny objects move slowly up the rock step which is near the final summit slope. Then the clouds closed in again. That, if it was really they, was the last that was ever seen of Mallory and Irvine. Nine years later one of their ice axes was found upon the mountain. Did they perish on the way up? Did they reach the summit and lose their lives on the way back down? No one knows.

The fourth British expedition, led by Hugh Ruttledge, came to Everest in 1933. Gales and blizzards harassed the party, but at last P. W. Harris and L. R. Wager were established in a new Camp VI placed at the tremendous height of 27,400 feet. About an hour's climb above the camp, they found the ice ax which must have belonged to Mallory or Irvine. Proceeding upward they reconnoitered the rock steps on the ridge but judged the difficulties there to be so great that they made the traverse on the north face much as Norton had done and, like him, reached a point a little above 28,100 feet before being forced to turn back. F. S. Smythe and Eric Shipton, in turn, occupied Camp VI and went on the same route toward the summit. When Shipton was unable to proceed, Smythe went on alone and reached about the same point as his predecessors, roughly one thousand feet short of the summit.

Three more expeditions went out in the next several years, a reconnaissance under Shipton in 1935, a climbing party led by Ruttledge in 1936, and another led by H. W. Tilman in 1938, but every serious attempt on the summit was beaten back, far short of the goal, by extremely bad weather.

Up to this point it was judged that the north side of the mountain offered the only feasible route to the summit, and the south side was held to be unclimbable. When political events north of the Himalayas indicated that it would become impossible to approach the mountain any longer from that side, attention turned to the hitherto little-known southern face. In 1951 Shipton led a new reconnaissance which approached Everest from the south and southwest. In 1952 the Swiss sent a Himalayan party to try to climb the mountain from that side. They made two attempts, the first at the usual time in the spring before the monsoon, the latter in the fall after the monsoon. Both times their route was approximately the same. Marching across Nepal to Katmandu, they made base camp upon the Khumbu glacier at 17,225 feet. Establishing a series of higher camps, they went up the glacier, negotiated a difficult ice fall, climbed the

Western cwm,[1] a great hollow on the mountainside, ascended the glacier at the foot of Lhotse, the south peak of Everest, and came out finally on the South col of the main mountain. Putting a high camp on up at 27,550 feet, Raymond Lambert and the Sherpa porter Tenzing Norkay tried for the summit. Their highest point was 28,210 feet, reached on May 28, probably a little higher than anyone else had ever been on the mountain unless it was Mallory and Irvine. In the autumn very bad weather kept the party for some time below the South col; later, on the way up, a fall of ice took the life of one of the porters. Setting out from a camp a little ways above the South col, on November 20 Raymond Lambert, Ernest Reiss, and the Sherpa Tenzing climbed to approximately 26,686 feet. Encountering gales with a velocity of seventy miles per hour and temperatures which fell to 40 degrees below zero, they were obliged to retreat. Conferring with Gabriel Chevalley, the leader of the expedition, it was decided that nothing more could be accomplished that year and, in a blizzard which turned the Western cwm into an inferno of seething snow, the party withdrew from the mountain.

In the summer of 1953 the British resumed the attack on Everest. The leader of the expedition was John Hunt, and the approach was again from the south, using in general the same route which had been reconnoitered by Shipton and followed by the Swiss. Equipment used took advantage of previous experience on the highest mountain in the world and included improved oxygen apparatus. Hunt pointed out that if and when the victory was finally won, the climbers who first attained the summit of Everest would also stand, as it were, at the apex of a pyramid of hard-won experience. He said: "The triumph will be shared by all who have helped to build it."

Climbing the Western cwm and the Lhotse glacier much as the Swiss had done, the British placed their Camp VIII on the South col at 27,000 feet. Toiling up the steep ridge above, they established the final assault camp at 27,900 feet. From here at 6:30 o'clock on the morning of May 29 two men, using oxygen, moved toward the summit, Edmund Hillary of New Zealand, and the Sherpa porter, Tenzing Norkay. The snow underfoot was soft and unstable, but

[1]The word "cwm," which has come to be applied to this bowl on the side of Everest, is of Welsh origin and is pronounced "koom."

by nine o'clock they had climbed to the South summit of the mountain. Above was a steep snow-covered ridge. On the right side of the ridge, cornices of ice overhung the 12,000 foot drop of that side of the mountain; on the left, the snow descended to the rock precipices which arose from the Western cwm. Cutting steps in the steep, hard snow between the cornices and the precipices, the two men proceeded steadily upward. A vertical face of rock forty feet high barred the way, but was surmounted by climbing a narrow crack between the rock and the attached cornice. The ridge still rose relentlessly above them, and they went on cutting steps upward. But at last the ridge ran up to a sharp point, and then dropped away. It was 11:30 in the morning, and Hillary and Tenzing were standing on the ultimate summit of the highest mountain in the world.

The fact that it was a Britisher and a Sherpa who thus shared this great triumph is significant. It is climbers from the West who have inspired and conducted such expeditions as the present chapter has described, but they themselves have often paid tribute to the native porters and guides, Bhutias, Gurkhas, and specially Sherpas, admiringly called "Tigers," who have gone with them to the heights. Of all these men it is the Sherpa Tenzing Norkay to whom the greatest fame attaches not only for his final victory with Hillary on Everest but also for his many exploits ever since he first began climbing with Shipton in 1935. Just before Tenzing left on his second trip to Everest with the Swiss in the fall of 1952, the following account of him was given by his close friend Dhanbakhat Rai of Darjeeling:

I will tell you about Tenzing. I speak with him and this is what he say. His name is Tenzing Norkay (Sherpa) and he was born at Solo Khumboo, which is in East Nepal, in June 1914.

The name of his village is Khumjun and it is not so big but quite comfortable, and there are beautiful sights to see around there. His home is within that particular place where there are many Sherpas who have lived there a long time. And Tenzing is one of these Sherpas who live there to gaze and feel the cold places. His house is near the village.

His father is Mingma and his mother Kingium. He has relations in his native place and at Toongsung Busti in Darjeeling. His two elder brothers are already expired and three elder sisters still live at his native place. Sadly his father died last year.

Tenzing came to Darjeeling in 1933 and married a girl of our town. His son is already expired but he has got two daughters. Though he is an uneducated man he

148

wants the future fortune of his daughters to be glorious so he is having them educated at the Nepali Girls' School in Darjeeling.

It was many years ago that Tenzing used to pay interest to the stories of mountain expedition from his parents and grandparents. When he grew up he was mindful to climb the mountain. So he fled away from his home along with his friends, and they were introduced to some climbers in Darjeeling as porters. His first expedition was with Mr. Eric Shipton in 1935, to Everest. It lasted for six months and they climbed up to 24,000 feet. There were one hundred Sherpa porters and ten Englishmen. They found the body of Mr. Wilson who went to climb Everest without permission in 1934, along with two porters whose bodies they also found. In 1936 he again went with Ruglitch [Ruttledge] along with fifty porters and twelve Englishmen to Everest and they climbed to 24,000 feet. [Here follow details of numerous other expeditions in which Tenzing participated.]

In 1952 he climbed with the Swiss expedition on Everest again. They reached up to 28,210 feet and Tenzing he say that if he would have provided enough foodstuff they could have climbed to the summit. Even he say a cup of tea would make him to reach the top, but alas, they had no any foodstuff. Tenzing he went up there without using the oxygen gas. Dr. Weiss and he though they have no food went upwards, but they could walk only one minute and rest five. Two Swiss climbers and three Sherpas already returned from 25,000 feet, as they could not climb up. A wonderful flower had been found in 28,000 feet colored yellow without any leaves and branches. Tenzing he also say that when he spit it becomes snow and falls as a stone. When they breathe from mouth the vapor becomes snow and sticks to their moustache and hair. On fourth September of this year Tenzing he leaves Darjeeling for the climbing of Everest with the Swiss expedition. They will begin to climb in October and it will last three months. When it is finished he will come to live with his daughters.

Though he is uneducated, Tenzing say he is quite experienced about climbing the mountains. Sometimes he guides the climbers and always he can describe about the climbing in detail, as now his experiences are matured. Tenzing he gets 225 rupees as monthly pay and three rupees per day as snow allowances. He gets free food and clothes, but there is nothing about his insurance.

Tenzing he likes very much to climb the mountains and feels much happy to reach the highest point of earth and being one of only living person to do so. He does not care anything but he keeps aim only to reach the summit. He feels nothing for October climb but to get on top of the peak. But one thing he say, and that is when he reaches in the middle of the mountain, above 16,000 feet, he does not feel hungry or thirsty or fear of anything. Neither he can remember his family or home nor any danger. Only he thinks to reach the summit. Such is the feeling in his mind.

Tenzing is a handsome man with laughing face. He is very honest and amicable and his manners and behavior are good. He can understand some of the English words and easily understands Nepali. He is a tall fellow, about five feet eight inches in height and his complexion is mixed with white and rosy color.

This is what he say to me. This is what I tell you about him.[1]

Despite differences of race and nation, there is surely a kinship of spirit among Mallory who wanted to climb Everest "because it is there," Hillary who achieved the goal his predecessor was denied, Tenzing who likes "to gaze and feel the cold places," and many others in both the East and the West who love the great mountains.

---

[1] *The Statesman* (Calcutta), September 14, 1952.

11 Power

of Religion

Many religions are at home in India. Hinduism, Jainism, Buddhism, and Sikhism originated there; Christianity, Zoroastrianism, and Islam were introduced from the outside; and various tribal religions are still adhered to by numerous primitive peoples. Statistics on these religions have recently been published from the 1951 census.[1] Applying the reported percentages to the population of 356,829,485 persons in India proper, exclusive of Jammu and Kashmir and the tribal areas of Assam, the following figures may be tabulated:

Religion	Per Cent of Population of India	Number of Adherents
Hinduism	84.99	303,269,379
Islam	9.93	35,433,168
Christianity	2.30	8,207,078
Sikhism	1.74	6,208,833
Tribal	0.48	1,712,782
Jainism	0.45	1,605,733
Buddhism	0.06	214,098
Zoroastrianism	0.03	107,049
Miscellaneous	0.02	71,365
	100.00	356,829,485

[1]P. Oomman Philip in *The Christian Century*, LXX, 29, July 22, 1953, pp. 848-849.

In Chapter III on the history of India something has already been said about the origin or introduction of most of these religions, and in the following chapter Christianity will be further dealt with. The purpose of the present chapter is to record some salient aspects of the present life of these religions, particularly of those which are native to India, and to show how the recent events in Indian history have influenced them and how they are participating in what is transpiring there now.

As we saw in discussing the Hindu Code Bill, the four religions of Hinduism, Buddhism, Sikhism, and Jainism, are all considered essentially "Hindu." Since they arose on Indian soil, they belong to India in the closest possible way. Although there is no state religion in India, since the constitution guarantees the freedom of all religions, these four are in effect the national faiths. By the very etymology of the word, Hinduism is the religion of the Hindus as India is their land. Depending upon the point of view, Jainism and Buddhism may be called heresies or reformations, but at any rate they are movements which arose within Hinduism and only gradually attained the status of separate religions. Sikhism combined elements of Hinduism and Islam, but was repudiated so violently by the Muslims as to be driven back into closer relationships with Hinduism. As shown by the statistics cited above, the adherents of Hinduism, Sikhism, Jainism, and Buddhism constitute 87.24 per cent of the population of India. Thus the four "Hindu" religions are not only those native to India, but also those to which in fact the enormous majority of its people belong.

The achievement of Indian independence was accomplished only through a strong development of national feeling, and was naturally accompanied by a powerful new emphasis upon everything Indian. In secular life an illustration of this fact is the constitutional requirement, already mentioned elsewhere, that English be replaced by Hindi as the official national language within fifteen years. There is still vigorous debate over the wisdom of this move; yet the country is proceeding rapidly in the direction determined upon. At many a railroad station the English name of the town has been painted out and the name is given only in Hindi or perhaps in the language of the particular state, for example, Bengali. University examinations are already being set in Hindi, and colleges are transferring instruction from English to that language as rapidly as possible. In spite of the fact that a very extensive literature in scientific and other subjects thereby becomes inaccessible to students, it is held important above all else that a nation should live by its own national language. In the area of religion, by a similar logic, there has been a new emphasis upon the faiths which are native to India. The "Hindu" religions have in fact experienced a revival. Evidences of their increased vitality will appear in the following descriptions of their present life.

Hinduism cannot be described in terms of a creed or a fixed set of dogmas, for it is by nature flexible and inclusive. That which is rigid about it is caste, a stratification of the society of those who belong to it. The hypothetical origin of caste in India has been dealt with earlier in this book. Here we may recall the description of the duties of the four main castes given by the Bhagavad Gita: "Control of the mind, control of the senses, austerity, cleanliness, forbearance, and uprightness, as also knowledge, realization, and faith—these are the duties of a Brahman, born of his own nature. Heroism, high spirit, firmness, resourcefulness, dauntlessness in battle, generosity, and sovereignty—these are the duties of a Kshatriya, born of his own nature. Agriculture, cattle-rearing, and trade are the duties of a Vaisya, born of his own nature. And the duty of a Sudra, born of his own nature, is action consisting of service."

In belief, Hinduism teaches that Brahman is the soul of the universe. Impersonal and unknowable as Brahman is, it yet manifests itself in and may be contemplated through such deities or symbols as Brahma, Vishnu, Śiva, Kali, Durga, and others. Indeed, it is taught that whenever goodness fails and evil prevails, the supreme god is born in some new form on earth to establish righteousness and punish the unrighteous. Thus Hinduism recognizes many incarnations of the divine, and not only in India but also in other lands. Fundamentally the soul of the individual is one with the soul of the universe, but the path to the liberating recognition of this truth is long and hard, requiring many reincarnations. In the endeavor to attain unitive knowledge of the divine, there are different methods which may be followed. Karmayoga is the way of right activity; Bhaktiyoga is the

manner of devoted love; Rajayoga calls for physical discipline and mental concentration; Jnanayoga is the way of philosophical speculation which emphasizes reason and intuition. Even the ways advocated by other religions are recognized as valid by Hinduism, for the Bhagavad Gita states that all religions are strung on the Lord like pearls on a necklace. Thus Hinduism believes in tolerance and mutual respect, and repudiates the attempt of any religion to make proselytes of the adherents of another.

The everyday practices of popular Hinduism may be witnessed by a visit to Hindu temples and seen in various festivals. The temple of Kalighat in Calcutta, from which the name of India's largest city is said to have been derived, may be presumed to be representative. Kalighat is in the southern part of Calcutta, not far from a water channel which connects with the River Hooghly, itself a branch of the Ganges. Accordingly, the temple enjoys proximity to sacred water.

153

The reason the temple stands at this particular spot is, according to myth, that when Kali, a wife of Śiva, was cut in pieces by the disk of Vishnu and at the order of the gods, one of her fingers fell here. The first temple is said to have been built 350 years ago, and 194 acres of land have been set aside for the maintenance of the institution. The temple building is not notable architecturally, nor is it possible to get too good a view of it, so crowded are the surroundings. Indeed the chief impression made upon the visitor from the West is of incredible confusion, dirt, and noise. Since Kali is regarded as terrible in character, it is thought that she must be propitiated with blood, and goats are sacrificed for that purpose in the temple area in great numbers. The corpses of the slain animals may often be seen lying in the courtyard long afterward. To this sanctuary comes a constant stream of worshipers, augmented to many thousands at special festivals. Guest hostels are adjacent for pilgrims. Not far away also are bathing and burning ghats.

Many Hindu festivals are observed during the course of the year. In Bengal the one of very greatest interest is the Durga Puja, or worship of Durga, which takes place in the autumn. Durga is another of the wives of Śiva, less ferocious in character than Kali. The myth upon which this worship is based concerns a time when the world was menaced by a demon of particularly dangerous and wily nature. When Durga undertook to combat the demon, the gods bestowed upon her their various attributes, and she is therefore portrayed with ten arms, holding as many symbols of the gods. Although the demon transformed himself into many shapes endeavoring to elude her, Durga was at last victorious over him, and the statues regularly show her in the act of plunging a sword into the breast of a horrible-visaged man who falls beneath her feet. This story is presumably taken quite literally by many of the common people; by others among the educated it is certainly regarded as an allegory. It is one illustration of the truth taught by Hinduism, that in every period of crisis the god becomes manifest on earth to destroy the evil. Even more broadly, it symbolizes the divine beneficence as it is particularly felt in nature in the beauty of the autumnal season. In whatever way it is interpreted, the festival of Durga is celebrated by a multitude of people

154

with much enthusiasm. All over Calcutta sheds and enclosures are erected at prominent street corners. In each there are elaborately fashioned images of Durga and accompanying deities. Sometimes the statues are patterned after the classical forms of Indian antiquity, sometimes they represent the liveliest play of present imagination. In general Durga is represented as a buxom and beautiful woman, and she is often garbed in bright-colored clothes. The offerings of the people, small gifts of food or flowers, are spread out in front of the goddess, and in her presence the priests burn incense, ring bells, and dance to the accompaniment of a small orchestra of drums and flutes. People visit these shrines in great numbers, remaining for a time in contemplation of the pageant set before them. Many seem casual, some appear touched by religious devotion. At the end of the period of the festival the statues are loaded into decorated trucks and these are driven through the streets of the city with much music and tumult. The destination is the river. There the images are set afloat

to drift out of sight upon the sacred waters as the goddess returns to her home. Similar festivals are observed in honor of Sarasvati, goddess of learning, and yet various other deities in the course of the year.

Another Hindu festival in this part of India is the annual pilgrimage to Sagar Island, which is at the mouth of the Hooghly River about seventy-five miles from Calcutta. Many thousands of people made the journey to this place in January, 1953, proceeding on crowded steamers and country boats, by equally crowded trains and buses, or on foot. There they bathed in the sea in the early morning, and then worshiped in the temple of Kapilmuni. The origin of the festival is explained as follows: Sagar Island is named for a king of that name who was the thirteenth ancestor of the Hindu hero and deity, Rama. Sagar performed the Aśvamedha or horse-sacrifice ninety-nine times. This ceremony consisted of sending a horse all around India with a challenge to any who dared to stop it. If the horse returned without having been held anywhere, it was a sign that all were acquiescent in the supremacy of the challenger. The animal was thereupon solemnly offered in sacrifice to the gods. When King Sagar made preparations to offer this sacrifice for the one hundredth time, Indra, king of heaven, who had himself repeated the ceremony on one hundred occasions, was made jealous. Indra stole the horse, therefore, and hid it in the subterranean cell of the sage Kapilmuni. When the 60,000 sons of Sagar traced the horse to this hiding place they assumed that Kapilmuni was responsible for the theft and assaulted the holy man. He, roused from the meditation in which he had been immersed, opened his eyes and uttered a curse upon his attackers. Forthwith they were burned to ashes and consigned to hell. When a grandson of Sagar came to Kapilmuni in search of his father and uncles and learned what had happened, he begged the saint to redeem the souls of the dead. Kapilmuni replied that this could be done only if the waters of Ganga could be led to the spot and brought in contact with the ashes. The goddess Ganga was still at that time residing in heaven in the custody of the god Brahma. The grandson of Sagar prayed to Brahma about the matter but died before his supplication was effective. His son in turn continued the entreaty, and at last Brahma allowed Ganga to visit the earth. A guide was able to indicate only part of the way to the necessary spot. Ganga, therefore, in order to make sure of coming to the exact place, divided herself into a hundred mouths, and thus the delta of the Ganges was formed. One of these mouths reached the cell of Kapilmuni, washed the ashes of the slain sons of King Sagar, and thereby made it possible for their souls to be admitted to heaven. So it was that Ganga became the sacred river of a hundred mouths, and Sagar Island became a celebrated place of Hindu pilgrimage.

The foregoing are concrete examples of what orthodox Hinduism teaches and of how it functions in the everyday lives of its adherents at the present time. As one observes the priests in their rituals and the devotees in their pilgrimages and ablutions, there can be no doubt that this religion has deep roots and is being promulgated with new authority and practiced with new fervor against the background of India's recent national awakening.

There is also a reformed type of Hinduism which must be considered. It arose in the nineteenth century, in part as a revulsion against the crudities of orthodox Hinduism, in part under the influence of Christianity and as a reaction to the impact of that faith. An early leader of the movement was Ram Mohan Roy. He was born a Brahman, and enjoyed privileges of wealth and culture. Even in his youth he was repelled by the idolatry of orthodox Hinduism and revolted by the custom of *sati*, the burning of widows on the funeral pyres of their husbands. Wandering in India, he studied Buddhism, and going to England he learned Hebrew and Greek and came under Christian influence. The teachings of the Vedas and Upanishads remained, however, his chief source of inspiration, and in their monistic doctrine of one world-spirit he found something which transcended polytheism and idolatry. In 1828 he founded a religious society called the Brahmo Samaj, or House of God. It was open to all without regard to caste or race or nationality, and taught the universalism of true religion. The famous Tagore family joined the movement, and the sect still exists although on a very small scale today.

The next and the greatest leader of reformed Hinduism was Ramakrishna. He was born eight years after the founding of the Brahmo Samaj, and like Ram Mohan Roy was also a Brahman but of a poor family. For many years he worshiped the goddess Kali, whom he considered "the Mother," with the most ardent and strenuous devotion. In the course of his religious exercises he had a great many experiences of trance and mystical illumination of the most extreme and remarkable sort. His place of meditation was in the temple of Dhakina Kali at Dhakineswar on the Hooghly six miles from Calcutta. As his fame spread, large numbers of young men came there

to see him and listen to his teachings. To them he enunciated the doctrines of Hinduism in an exalted form and as agreeing with and embracing the fundamental truths of all the great religions of the world. Before he died in 1886, there came to him a boy named Narendranath Dutt who was destined to carry his teachings widely abroad. The family from which the youth came had belonged to the Brahmo Samaj, and he himself had attended a Christian mission school. With this background he readily became an ardent disciple of Ramakrishna. Later known as the Swami Vivekananda, he traveled to the United States in 1893 to attend the Parliament of Religions which was held at the World's Fair in Chicago. Although he arrived quite unannounced and without credentials, after an extemporaneous address of remarkable character he became the sensation of the meeting. On his return journey he also taught in England, on the Continent, and elsewhere. His greatest contribution was the organization of the Ramakrishna Mission, to the success of which his own popularity contributed much. It is said that he inspired the launching of the Mission on a Christmas Eve by telling the story of Jesus. Today the Ramakrishna Mission is reported to have twelve centers in the

United States, and sixty-six monasteries and missions in India as well as a number of dispensaries, hospitals, clinics, reading rooms, and other institutions which testify to its interest in the social application of its teachings. The temple of Belur Math, on the river not far from Dhakineswar, is an important center of the Mission. Founded by Swami Vivekananda it is said to have been built largely by gifts from the United States. It is a beautiful building set in quiet grounds. In the city of Calcutta the Ramakrishna Mission also has a Cultural Institute which conducts a series of public Sunday evening lectures and forums on a great variety of subjects.

In the present time, reformed Hinduism has taken on the role of protagonist of the "spirituality" of the East against the "materialism" of the West. In the annual retreat of the Ramakrishna Mission at Suri in the fall of 1952, an American guest speaker was put on the program immediately after an Indian speaker who devoted his address largely to an attack upon the materialism of the United States. On the other hand, one of the forums of the Ramakrishna Cultural Institute in Calcutta was given to consideration of the place of women in American life, following a program on the place of women in Indian life, and the presentation by a group of American women was received appreciatively.

In the positive statement of its message, the Ramakrishna Mission endeavors to show the relevance of its teachings to the present problems of India. As an example may be cited a meeting held at Dhakineswar on January 1, 1953. The occasion was the anniversary of the event on January 1, 1886, when Ramakrishna appeared before his followers as Kalpataru or the "fulfiller of all wishes," and was recognized by them as an incarnation of God. The chief speaker at the Dhakineswar gathering was a well-known Bengali writer, Sri Achintya Kumar Sen Gupta. He declared that Ramakrishna was a never-failing fountain of nectar, whose words would continue to reverberate as long as the world lasted and infuse new life into all seekers after truth. Ramakrishna, the speaker went on, was born into one faith but practiced the methods of many different religions and emerged with the conclusion that God is one, by whatever names he may be called. Since everything, inanimate as well as animate, is an embodiment of God, all things are equal, and thus the teaching of Ramakrishna was a statement of the highest form of socialism. Ramakrishna worshiped God as the Mother, who is not distant but very near at hand, indeed within one. To know that God is omnipresent is the highest truth. The presiding officer at the same meeting was Sri Charu Chandra Biswas, government Minister for Law and Minority Affairs. He said that the appearance of Ramakrishna at a time when Bengali Hindu society was in a state of confusion toward the close of the last century, was a great benefit because he saved Hindu religion and culture from decay and abandonment. Since he dedicated his life to the cause of national resurrection, Ramakrishna was truly one of the national heroes of India.

Buddhism is a religion which seems devoid of the most characteristic mark of religion, belief in God or gods. Gautama Buddha did not deny, indeed, that there are many gods, goddesses, and demons in the universe, but to him they, too, like man, were finite beings, subject to death and rebirth, and he did not pray to them. Nevertheless the cosmic order itself, pervaded and controlled by the great law of karma, holds for all practical purposes the place of supreme deity, and Buddhism, professing knowledge of this order, offers to man a message of redemption and salvation. The teaching of Buddhism may be said to begin with a doctrine of causality: all phenomena are links in a causal series. When life, therefore, is found to be characterized by misery, transience, and ultimate unreality, it is evident that there must be some cause for this ill. Upon analysis, the cause is found to lie in ignorance which leaves man bound by his evil desires and his very thirst for existence. As for man himself, he is indeed but a temporary assemblage of constituent parts including his body and various aspects of his consciousness. All of these are constantly changing, and at death they fall quite apart. Nevertheless, if desire has not been eradicated, karma will bring about the assembling of a new set of aggregates and a further existence will result, bearing the stamp of the former. But by following the noble path of right understanding, right conduct, and right concentration outlined by Buddhism, it is possible to root out all unworthy desire and escape into the passionless peace of nirvana. As it is stated in the writings of Buddhism: "Look-

161

ing for the maker of this tabernacle [of the self] I shall have to run through a course of many births, so long as I do not find it, and painful is birth again and again. But now, maker of the tabernacle, thou hast been seen; thou shalt not make up this tabernacle again. All thy rafters are broken, thy ridgepole is sundered; the mind approaching nirvana has attained extinction of all desires." The one who attains this goal becomes an arhat and is "worthy." When he dies, he will be "extinguished like a lamp." This does not necessarily mean annihilation but rather entry into a state so transcendent that the Buddha himself is reported to have declined to say whether after death the arhat exists or does not exist. Upon these fundamental principles are erected the elaborated doctrines of the various schools of Buddhism. These include the late and northern form of Buddhism known as Mahayana or "great vehicle," in which it is taught that there are many Bodhisattvas, great spiritual beings destined for enlightenment and able even now to enter nirvana, who out of compassion remain in the world to assist other creatures toward deliverance.

While Buddhism is far stronger in many other countries than in the land of its origin, and in 1951 counted as adherents in India only the very small percentage of the population indicated at the beginning of this chapter, it is by no means a negligible force in the Indian scene and appears to be growing rather than losing in influence at the present time. In particular, the modern Buddhist organization, the Mahabodhi Society of India, launched by the late Venerable Anagarika Dharmapala and now presided over by Dr. Syama Prasad Mookerjee, has done much to save the religion from the extinction with which it appeared to be threatened and to revive it again as a vital force in India. It is pointed out by the leaders of the movement that Buddhism stands for the welfare of all men and for peace on earth, ideals to which India today is strongly devoted. This character of the religion was stressed, for example, in an article by Sri R. Barua in the journal of the Society, *The Maha Bodhi*, in the issue dated August, 1952, of the Christian Era, 2496 of the Buddhist Era.[1] He declared: "Buddhism is neither an esoteric doctrine, nor a sectarian religion, nor even a religion of a particular class, caste, community or nation, nor

[1] The Mahabodhi Society accepts the dates of 624-544 B.C. for the life of the Buddha.

is it bounded by time or space. On the contrary, it is essentially a religion of man, preached by a man for the amelioration and all round uplift and ultimate salvation of man."

In 1952 an event conducted by the Mahabodhi Society attracted a great deal of notice and was used as an occasion for calling attention to the relevance of the Buddhist message to the present aspirations of India. This was the re-enshrinement of the relics of Sariputta and Moggallana, the chief disciples of the Buddha. Supposed fragments of their bones, enclosed in caskets bearing their names, were discovered in 1851 by General Cunningham under one of the ancient stupas at Sanchi and sent to the British Museum in London. In 1949 they were returned to India and after being exhibited in different parts of the country and as far away as Burma and Cambodia, were placed on display in the Sri Dharmarajika Vihara, a Buddhist center in Calcutta. From there they were taken in November, 1952, back to Sanchi for

163

re-enshrinement.   The procession which took the relics from the vihara to Howrah Station at Calcutta was a mile in length.   A jeep was decorated to represent the white elephant which Maya Devi, the Buddha's mother, saw in a dream before he was born.   In the howdah sat Dr. Soft, the vice-president of the Mahabodhi Society, holding the relics.   The special train in which the relics were conveyed to Sanchi, carried also 250 Buddhist delegates from China, Burma, Ceylon, Pakistan, Sikkim, Nepal, and Tibet.   At Sanchi a new vihara, consisting of a stupa with a prayer hall in front, had been erected to receive the sacred objects.   The dome of the stupa was fashioned after the dome of the great Sanchi stupa, and the light-red stones used in the construction were of the same sort as those employed by ancient Buddhist builders.   Prime minister Nehru carried the relics up the steps of this building and handed them to two leading Buddhist priests, while many other yellow-robed monks rang bells, blew conches, and chanted the five precepts of the Buddha—to abstain from killing, from stealing, from wicked love, from lying, and from drink.   Addressing a crowd of 50,000 people, Mr. Nehru called upon the world to adopt the principles of the Buddha—love, tolerance, and compassion—for the solution of individual and international problems.   Citing the example of the famous Buddhist king Aśoka who relinquished the sword for the weapons of love, he said that the selection of the Aśoka wheel for the national flag and of the Aśoka lions for the national emblem was a deliberate expression of the sincere desire of India to work for good will and peace.   Dr. Mookerjee, president of the Mahabodhi Society, said in his address: "Gautama Buddha was not born on the soil of India by accident.   The genius of India, from time immemorial has been reflected through the words and deeds of mighty men, sages, and savants who gave to their country and to the world the benefits of their wisdom and guidance consistent with the changing needs and aspirations of society.   Gautama Buddha represented 2,500 years ago, a unique challenge of the scientific spirit of man when he declared his unwillingness to accept anything as true without a full and searching analysis and self-satisfaction.   He gave the world his message of love, peace, and understanding in a simple manner which carried faith and conviction not only to the learned but also to the masses of the

164

people. It gave solace and strength to millions throughout the world and it needed no sword to spread this doctrine to countries far and near."

Sikhism is a combination of elements from Hinduism and Islam, but is acceptable to neither, and constitutes an independent community which is one of the largest in India outside of those two religions. Its fundamental doctrines are found in the Granth Sahib or Noble Book, which contains the words of Guru Nanak (A.D. 1469-1538) and other early teachers. From Islam, Sikhism derives a strong monotheism, and from Hinduism it accepts the ideas of karma and transmigration. God is one, and instead of calling him by such limiting designations as Allah, Vishnu, Śiva, Rama, or Krishna, he is known simply as the True Name or the True Guru. While he rules over the world with inscrutable wisdom and predestines all creatures to their appointed ends, he is also immanent in everything and may be found within the heart of man. By meditation on the fact of God and endless repetition of his name, man may be absorbed into his reality and thus escape the round of rebirths. Since this is the way of salvation, neither the ritual observances of the Muslims nor the pilgrimages, ablutions, and idol worship of the Hindus can avail anything. In the sight of God all men are equal, and Sikhs are taught to live with their fellows as brothers. Whoever comes to a Sikh temple, of any race or caste or creed, may obtain hospitality.

In spite of an early heritage of pacifism, when Sikhism encountered the persecution of the Mughal emperors in the seventeenth and eighteenth centuries it took on a militant aspect which it has maintained ever since. Under the tenth Guru, Gobind Singh, who headed the movement from A.D. 1675 to 1708, the Sikhs were reorganized into a military theocracy known as the Khalsa. Members marked their adherence by wearing the five "k's" which are still the identifying marks of a Sikh: the *kesh*, long hair wound into a topknot; the *kangha*, a comb in the hair; the *kara*, a bracelet of steel; the *kachch*, a pair of shorts; and the *kirpan*, a two-edged dagger.

Under the special conditions of India's recent struggle for freedom from foreign oppression and of her present endeavor to build a new society in which all will have equality, the Sikhs have laid fresh emphasis upon the significance and relevance of their traditions of militancy and sacrifice for their country, and of their teachings of the oneness of all men. On December 23, 1952, the birthday of Guru Gobind Singh was celebrated in India. In Calcutta a long and colorful procession was staged by the large Sikh community. Bands, swordsmen, horsemen, banners, trucks bearing shrines for the Granth, and marching men and women went by. In the literature which was distributed on this occasion Gobind Singh was called a sage, scholar, and patriot; a rebel against tyranny and against social and religious oppression; an invincible hero with the sword and a glorious martyr. It was told how his birth coincided with the worst phase of Mughal tyranny, and how he played a mighty part in the drama of resistance. Suffering and self-immolation were already the traditional badge of his ancestors. His great-grandfather, Guru Arjun, the great apostle of truth and nonviolence, had to pay with his life for his glowing love of country and at the command of Emperor Shah Jahan was put to death at Lahore in a peculiarly cruel manner. Gobind's father, Guru Teg Bahadur, too, for the same offense of patriotism and sympathy with the weak and the oppressed, met with a similar fate and was beheaded in Delhi by the Emperor Aurangzib. Two of the younger sons of Guru Gobind Singh were buried alive in the Punjab for refusal to accept Islam, and two older sons died on the battlefield while fighting against the emperor's forces for the liberation of their oppressed homeland. Guru Gobind Singh himself experienced exile, and finally laid down his life in battle for the cause of his motherland. That the tyranny of the Mughal empire was finally uprooted was due in part to his efforts. After a recital along these lines of the chief facts in the life of the famous Guru, the Sikh literature invited all the inhabitants of Calcutta, irrespective of caste and creed, to join in the celebration of the birth "of one of the greatest martyrs of all times, who sacrificed his all for the sake of his country." In the procession, one of the many banners carried this typical Sikh slogan: "He who looks on all men as equals is religious."

The homeland of the Sikhs was in the Punjab, and when it was divided in 1947 between Pakistan and India most of them fled into India. In view of their patriotic traditions, it is not difficult to understand the protests which they made against the division or the appeals which they have voiced since that time for a separate state of their own.

Jainism, like Buddhism, is a movement which arose within Hinduism but attained distinct status. Like Buddhism, too, it looks back to a founder, Mahavira, who made a great renunciation of the goods of life and finally reached the liberation he was seeking. In fashion similar to Buddhism, also, Jainism is atheistic in the sense that it considers the gods of Hinduism to be finite beings and makes no prayer to them. But it recognizes a series of great conquerors, of whom Mahavira was only the last, who have won final victory over the ills of life, and it erects statues of them in its sanctuaries. All the universe, according to Jainism, is divided into living beings and nonliving matter. When the living comes into contact with the nonliving, karma takes its start, and karmic matter flows into the soul. As the soul becomes more and more full of matter, it sinks into deeper and deeper bondage; only if karma is progressively destroyed can the soul rise toward liberation. The ultimate state of desired freedom is that of a Siddha, more exalted than an arhat, who dwells in the realm of Ishatpragbhara at the top of the universe. Devoid of qualities or relationships of any sort, the soul there enjoys perfect bliss. A Jaina text states: "The liberated is not long nor small . . . neither heavy nor light . . . he is without body, without resurrection, without contact with matter, he is not feminine nor masculine nor neuter; he perceives, he knows, but there is no analogy [whereby to know the nature of the liberated soul]; its essence is without form; there is no condition of the unconditioned."

Since the universe is full of souls struggling toward liberation, the fundamental principle of Jaina ethics is to destroy no living thing. Known as *ahimsa*, this doctrine of the nonkilling of any form of life is carried to its logical extreme in Jainism. A monk sweeps the path before him lest he crush any tiny creature, and breathes through a cloth lest he inhale some insect. Rest homes are provided for aged and diseased animals where they are kept and fed until they die. Not to destroy life is, however, only the first of a number of vows which are enjoined upon the adherents of this faith. Others are not to speak untruth, not to steal, and not to own property. The last in-

167

junction is taken so seriously by the Digambara or "sky-clad" sect that the monk wears no clothes; among the Śvetambara or "white-clad" group this is modified to permit simple attire. For the lay adherents of the faith the severely ascetic rules of the monks are much relaxed, yet the ultimate aim is the same, to lead to the freeing of the soul from its entanglement with matter. In practice the rule against taking life has kept the Jains out of such occupations as agriculture and fishing, and has turned them to careers in business, law, and other such fields. In these areas they have prospered and thus, paradoxically enough, the members of a world-renouncing religion have risen to a favored position in the Indian social order. This is reflected in the beauty of their temples, from the exquisite white marble sanctuaries built long ago by Jaina bankers on Mount Abu to the colorful modern structures in the gardens of Badridas in Calcutta, and is seen also in the richness of thrones, temple replicas, and other objects of gold and silver customarily carried in Jaina religious processions.

Relatively small, self-contained, and wealthy, the community of Jains has been perhaps less stirred by the upsurge of nationalism than the other religions dealt with above. Yet the general awakening of interest in the Indian cultural and religious heritage which has marked the end of the nineteenth and first half of the twentieth centuries has definitely been shared by the Jains. Societies have been formed for the publication of the sacred texts of the religion, gazettes and periodicals have been issued, and the Young Men's Jaina Association has been organized in northern and southern India. This religion also helped to determine the manner in which India's struggle for independence was carried out. There were many Jains in Western India where Gandhi grew up, and their doctrine of *ahimsa* was unquestionably influential in the shaping of his own conception of nonviolence, an idea to which he said he had been devoted from as early a time as he could remember. And the Jains continue to desire to have a government animated by the spirit of their religion and dedicated to the principles of love and respect for life.

These, then, to use the language of the Hindu Code Bill are the "Hindu" religions, Hinduism, Buddhism, Sikhism, and Jainism. They originated in India, they have been a part of the life of the land for a long time and, naturally enough, they have been in one way or another and to a greater or lesser degree particularly close to the nationalistic movement of recent days. Caught up in the upsurge of renewed and increased interest in everything Indian, they have on the whole experienced revival and become more powerful forces.

Of the faiths which were introduced from the outside, Zoroastrianism is presumably the most compatible with the "Hindu" religions. The ultimate source of the religion of Zoroaster was the same as that of the Vedic Aryans. The original heritage of the Aryans who settled in Iran as of the Aryans who came into India was the nature worship of their common ancestors. Language reveals the relationship of the two groups, as well as their differentiation. The Aryans of Iran worshiped the gods Mithra and Haoma; the Aryans of India did reverence to Mitra and Soma. In Iran the gods were *ahuras* and the demons *devas;* in India the good deities were *devas* and the evil spirits *asuras.* The prophet Zarathushtra, whose name is more familiar in the Greek form Zoroaster, taught that Ahura Mazda, the Wise Lord, was the supreme god, but held too that this deity had been opposed from the beginning of the world by the evil spirit, Angra Mainyu. He also expected, however, that at the end of the world there would be a fiery judgment in which Ahura Mazda would destroy all evil and bestow welfare and immortality upon faithful men. Whether Zoroaster lived around 500 or 600, or even 1000 B.C., remains uncertain, but we know that he still had many followers in Persia when the Muslims conquered that land in the seventh century A.D. Under the impact of Islam, most of the Zoroastrians fled, in the next century or two, to India. Settling there for the most part in Bombay and vicinity, in spite of their kinship with the Aryan Indians they remained a separate community.[1] Known as Parsis, even today their distinguishing dress includes the sacred shirt, girdle, and hat, which they claim as the ancient Aryan garb, going back to pre-Zoroastrian days. The girdle or cushti, a long piece of string woven of lamb's wool and wrapped three times around the waist, is interpreted as standing for the good thoughts, good words, and good deeds

---

[1]Four fifths of the Zoroastrian Parsis still live in the state of Bombay, over half in the city of Bombay.

inculcated by Zoroaster. With this the child is formally invested when, after the age of seven, he is officially taken into the religion.

To the Zoroastrians, fire has long been a symbol and is personified as Atar, the son of Ahura Mazda. Zoroaster himself is said to have declared to Ahura Mazda, "At every offering of reverence to thy Fire, I will bethink me of Right so long as I have power," and at the last to have been slain while ministering before the sacred fire. And so until today in Zoroastrian temples a sacred fire is kept constantly burning. Priests, wearing a cloth over their mouths lest their breaths contaminate the flame, feed the fire with sandalwood and distribute the ashes to worshipers to rub upon their foreheads and eyelids. It is not the physical fire which is worshiped, modern Zoroastrians explain, it is the Inner Spiritual Fire, Ahura Mazda, who lights the faithful clearly through life. In Calcutta the Zoroastrian fire temple may be found on Metcalf Street, but non-Parsis are not admitted to the inner sanctuary.

Characteristic also of Zoroastrianism is the exposure of the dead to the vultures in "towers of silence," a practice which avoids the contamination of fire, soil, or water which would be involved in other methods of disposition of the corpse. At Calcutta the towers of silence of the small Parsi community are located far to the east of the city on Beliaghatta Main Road. Extensive gardens are well hidden

by a high, solid surrounding wall. Admitted through the main gate, the funeral procession advances first to the house of prayer, then goes on to the towers, themselves secluded behind an inner wall. The towers are powerfully built of masonry, and look something like gigantic wells. The larger and newer of the two was built in 1912 "at the sole expense of the Parsi Zoroastrian Anjuman of Calcutta," as an inscription records. The body of the deceased is laid upon a stone bench for the last farewell, then carried up the steps and deposited within the tower by the corpse-bearers who alone are allowed ever to enter there.

Upon their first arrival in India, the Parsis became farmers and small traders. Especially under British rule, showing themselves adaptable to Western customs and being unhampered by Hindu rules of caste and food, they progressed rapidly. Small as the total community is, they are recognized as leaders in industry and business, and also in social reform and political advancement. Outstanding is the name of J. N. Tata, a Parsi, who founded The Tata Iron and Steel Company Limited, probably the largest industry in the country today. In its advertisements this company stresses the great achievements of ancient India and points proudly to their counterparts in the present. Recalling that in the time of Aśoka, Indian seamen were making voyages of sixty days or more and that the discovery of the monsoon winds by Hippalus in A.D. 45 also brought trading fleets from the West to Indian ports, it is stated that Indian ships are once again on the high seas, carrying her merchandise to the markets of the world. Speaking of the ancient steel industry which produced the remarkable wrought-iron pillar erected by Kumara Gupta A.D. 415, still a source of wonder to scientists 1,500 years later, it is noted that, stimulated by a resurgence of genius and determination, Indian craftsmanship is now asserting itself afresh. In this Indian renaissance, it is declared, Tata Steel plays a vital part. And thus the vigorous faith of the Zoroastrian Parsis is active in the making of the new India.

Since its introduction in the eleventh century and later, the religion of Islam has played a large part in the history of the Indo-Pakistani subcontinent. The fundamentals of Islam as proclaimed by Muhammad, recorded in the Qur'an, and elaborated in the Hadith or tradition, can be plainly and briefly stated. The doctrines are belief in the one god Allah, in his angels, his divine books, his messengers, and in the last judgment. The practical duties are to recite the profession of faith: "There is no god but Allah, and Muhammad is the messenger of Allah"; to pray five times a day toward Mecca; to give alms; to fast, especially during the month of Ramadan; and

172

to make pilgrimage once in a lifetime, if possible, to Mecca. In its historical development, two chief groups took form within Islam. The Sunnites constitute the orthodox and majority party, devoted to the *sunnah* or "usage" of Muhammed as handed down in the tradition; the Shi'ites are the "following" of 'Ali, a cousin of Muhammad and husband of his daughter Fatimah, who was murdered in early dynastic struggles but is held by this group to be the head of a line of divinely appointed rulers, the last of whom is yet to reappear to inaugurate the millennium. In the Indo-Pakistani subcontinent prior to division, the majority of Muslims were Sunnites, approximately one out of thirteen was a Shi'ite. In its social teachings, Islam has long refused to recognize racial distinctions and has considered all Muslims equal before Allah without regard to any differences in the color of their skins. Polygamy is allowed, but Muslim law limits to four the number of wives a man may take; in fact, monogamy is often the practice. The institution of purdah has also been very prominent in Indian Islam. The name is derived from the Hindi word *pardah*, meaning veil or curtain, and refers to the keeping of women in extreme seclusion, a practice still widely observed although modified in some quarters.

In the development of Islam on the Indo-Pakistani subcontinent, various special movements arose. Shah Wali Allah of Delhi (eighteenth century) taught social reform and influenced in that direction the famous Muslim seminary at Deoband which attained a position of prestige in the Muslim world second only to al Azhar seminary in Cairo. Sayyid Ahmad Khan (1817-1898) worked for the modernization and westernization of Islam, and to that end founded the Muhammadan Anglo-Oriental College or Muslim University at Aligarh. Amir 'Ali (1849-1928), a Shi'ite and a judge of the Calcutta High Court, published books on *The Spirit of Islam* and other subjects which aimed to show the leadership Islam had historically exercised with regard to war, slavery, women, the scientific spirit, and democracy. Muhammad Iqbal (1876-1938), who was called the Poet of the East, condemned the customary Muslim ethic of resignation and called upon the followers of Muhammad to take vigorous action to change the lamentable plight of Indian Muslim society. Even an unbeliever who is dynamic and active is more righteous, he felt, than a Muslim whose religion consists only in passivity:

An infidel before his idol with wakeful heart
Is better than the religious man asleep in the mosque.

Ultimately the awakening of Islam was channeled largely into the cause of the Muslim League and the program which led to the creation of the state of Pakistan. In Pakistan in 1952 Muslims comprised 86 per cent of the population. In November, 1953, it was reported that the Constituent Assembly which was drafting the permanent constitution for Pakistan had voted that the nation shall become an "Islamic republic." Not only does the new constitution make Islam the religion of the state, it also directs the government to propagate the Muslim faith, makes only Muslims eligible for the presidency, and includes a provision that no law can be passed which is out of accord with the Qur'an.[1]

In India, nearly 10 per cent of the population is still Muslim as shown in the tabulation at the head of this chapter. In talking with individual Muslims still living in India, I found that they often expressed regret over the partition of the land and indicated the intention and desire to remain permanently in India unless driven out by disturbances. As faithful members of Islam they continue the practices of their religion as usual. In Calcutta, Nakhoda's Mosque is the largest place of Muslim worship. Above the main entrance of the mosque are six clock faces on which the hands are set to show the hours of prayer and of other services. At the top of the highest minaret is a public-address system which the muezzin uses to give the call to prayer. Inside, there are four prayer halls, one above the other, opening upon a vertical shaft which gives visual access to the prayer niche and pulpit. "Chicago" loud-speakers connected with the microphone at the pulpit provide for the amplification of the sermon. At the Friday preaching service it is said that upward of four thousand persons assemble. The sermon is in Arabic. One young Muslim, whose mother tongue is Urdu, states that he attends although he does not understand the words. There may be some

[1]*The Christian Century,* LXX, 47, November 25, 1953, p. 1348.

174

significance in the fact that the foreign language he is now learning is not Arabic but English.

Christianity, the other chief religion introduced into India from the outside, will be dealt with in the following chapter. This leaves what the census calls Tribal religion, to which according to the figures at the head of this chapter over 1,700,000 persons belong. In actuality we have here hundreds of different primitive religions still practiced in the more remote regions of India. In these areas change appears to wait upon the slow processes of education and the development of civilization.

To all of the religions of India the constitution of the land promises equal treatment. The "Hindu" religions are accorded no special privileges in law. The new India calls itself a secular state. By this it is not meant to disparage things spiritual, but it is meant that there is not going to be any state religion. Explaining the principle, Mr. Nehru said in parliament: "This does not mean that religion ceases to be an important factor in the private life of the individual. It means that the state and religion are not tied together.

It simply means the repetition of the cardinal doctrine of modern democratic practice, the separation of the state from religion, and the full protection of every religion." At least in theory, therefore, the native religions of Hinduism, Buddhism, Sikhism, and Jainism, and the religions which have been introduced into India from outside, Zoroastrianism, Islam, and Christianity, are all on exactly the same legal footing. In setting up safeguards for the rights of the citizens of India, the constitution provides that "the state shall not discriminate against any citizen on grounds only of religion"; that "all persons are equally entitled to freedom of conscience and the right freely to profess, practise and propagate religion"; and that "every religious denomination or any section thereof shall have the right to establish and maintain institutions for religious and charitable purposes."

It is plain, nevertheless, from the facts and trends noted in this chapter that the strong nationalism of modern India has had a stimulating effect upon the non-Christian religions in India and particularly upon those of the "Hindu" group, and that these religions are today very definitely a strong force with which to reckon in any consideration of Indian life. For the great majority of the Indian people, some kind of religion is an integral part of life, and for most of them that means one of the faiths which have been discussed in this chapter. In this connection it is significant that the Ecumenical Study Conference which was convened by the World Council of Churches at Lucknow, India, in December, 1952, and which dealt with the problems of the Christian Church in Asian lands, urged that Christian people need to increase their knowledge of the religion or religions by which they are surrounded and recommended the establishment of a school for the study of Hinduism and a school for the study of Buddhism to match the one which already exists for the study of Islam. The judgment was also expressed that when Christianity considers the great rival forces which it confronts in the world today, it must think not only of Communism, scientific humanism, and democratic utopianism, but also of the non-Christian religions— a conclusion which seems necessary and inescapable.

12 Place

of Christianity

According to ancient tradition, Christianity was first preached in India by the Apostle Thomas. In an apocryphal book called the *Acts of Thomas*, which was written in Syriac at Edessa in Mesopotamia about A.D. 200, it is narrated that the apostles of Christ cast lots to determine to which land each should go and that it fell to Thomas to preach in India. He was unwilling to go, but it was providentially arranged that he was purchased as a slave and carpenter by a merchant from India and taken thither to the court of King Gondophares. When Gondophares gave Thomas money to construct a palace, the apostle distributed the money to the poor and explained that the king's palace was being built in heaven. Finally the king and others were converted to Christianity, then Thomas left to preach in another kingdom where he suffered martyrdom. Legendary as this account obviously is, it may contain a kernel of historical truth. The name of King Gondophares was formerly known only from this source and it could be supposed that he was a fictitious character and the whole story a pure invention. Early in the present century, however, archeologists excavated the ancient city of Taxila in North India and found coins bearing the name of Gondophares, so it is evident that he was an actual historical ruler. The date of his rule was in the first half of the first century A.D., probably around A.D. 19-48. The fact that although he ruled in India he was himself a Parthian, and that Taxila was the center of an extensive Scytho-Parthian kingdom, can explain the statement of the church historian, Eusebius, that Thomas preached in Parthia.

The Syrian Church of Malabar in South India preserves a tradition that Thomas landed at Cranganore in A.D. 52, founded seven churches there on the west coast, and later went on to preach on the east coast where he suffered death at the hands of a Brahman. The place of his martyrdom is shown at Mylapore near Madras, although his bones are supposed to have been taken back later to Edessa. Again the accuracy of the narrative cannot now be determined with certainty, but the historical situation presupposed is entirely credible, for Cranganore was an important seaport of the first century, and many Roman coins have been found at various places in South India, thus proving the commercial contacts of that time with the West.

In A.D. 522 a merchant named Cosmas from Alexandria, Egypt, made a trip to India on account of which he was afterward surnamed Indicopleustes or the "Indian navigator." In later years he became a monk and wrote a book on *Christian Topography*. In it he says: "In the Malabar country also, where pepper grows, there are Christians, and in Calliana there is a bishop who comes from Persia where he was consecrated." Although alternative identifications are proposed for Calliana, one with Quilon in Travancore, another with Kalyan near Bombay, there is no doubt that the statement of Cosmas is proof of the existence of Christianity in South India in the early part of the sixth century.

The later history of the Syrian Church of South India is interrupted by gaps and marred by divisions. In the sixteenth century when the Portuguese settled in South India, Roman Catholic influence became strong, and in 1599 a representative of the Pope succeeded in bringing the Malabar Church under the authority of Rome, where it continued for some sixty years. Shortly after the middle of the

178

seventeenth century the majority of the Syrian Christians separated themselves again from Rome, but a section of the church continued in allegiance to Roman Catholicism. Early in the nineteenth century representatives of the Church Missionary Society of the Church of England came to Malabar and worked with the non-Roman Syrian Christians. At least partly as a result of the new influence, there was a movement for reformation in the Syrian Church. The result, however, was a fresh division. The larger body remained as the Syrian Church of Malabar, the smaller reformed group became the Mar Thoma Syrian Church. Although both churches hold the same theological doctrines and use the same liturgy of St. James, the Mar Thoma Church is characterized by its greater evangelical and missionary interest, a mark of which was the organization of an evangelistic association in 1888. There was hostility between the two churches at the time of the separation, but they seem to be upon relatively good terms with each other now although there is no apparent hope of reunion at this time. As a matter of fact, the Syrian Church of Malabar itself has become divided into two groups, the Jacobites who recognize the patriarch of Antioch as administrative head, and the Orthodox who recognize the Catholicos of Malabar as administrative head.

All together the Syrian Christians constitute a large and important part of the entire body of Christians in India. In Travancore-Cochin where their chief strength is concentrated, they constitute nearly 40 per cent of the total population, as compared with slightly more than 2 per cent of Christians in the population of India as a whole. The Roman Catholic Syrians are now the most numerous having approximately one million members; the Syrian Church of Malabar is next in size, claiming 800,000 adherents; and the Mar Thoma Syrian Church is numerically the smallest, with 200,000 believers. The Syrian Church has experienced many vicissitudes and yet it has also exercised Christian influence upon its surroundings. It is not an accident that in Travancore, where it is very strong, there is a literacy rate of over 60 per cent, far ahead of an estimated 18 per cent average for all India. Indeed the Mar Thoma Church now claims a 95 per cent literacy. In connection with the celebration in 1952 of the nineteen hundredth anniversary of the traditional landing of Thomas in India, Dr. C. E. Abraham, Principal of Serampore College and a leading church historian of the Mar Thoma Church, declared that "the Syrian Church is astir today with a new life," and elsewhere pointed in substantiation of the statement to the facts that the Syrian Church is entirely self-supporting, the Mar Thoma group now depending on voluntary giving only; that the evangelistic association of the Mar Thoma Church has been doing vigorous missionary work in and outside Travancore for fifty years, and that a missionary order of the Orthodox Church has brought 19,000 converts into that body in the past twenty-eight years; that there is a growing interest in the practical application of Christian principles as shown, for example, by the studies of social and economic problems by the Youth Christian Council of Action at Kottayam; and that there is interest in the ecumenical movement as evidenced by participation of representatives of both the Orthodox and Mar Thoma Churches in the gatherings of the World Council of Churches.

Roman Catholicism came to India with the Portuguese. In 1542, only forty-four years after Vasco da Gama first landed at Calicut, the great Roman Catholic missionary, Francis Xavier, arrived at Goa which had become the capital of Portugal's Eastern empire. Although Xavier remained in India only three years, his labors were unremitting and prodigious. He went up and down the coast, ringing a bell to call the people together, preaching in the villages and winning, it is said, 700,000 converts. Afterward he voyaged to Japan and China but, worn with his arduous toils, died on December 2, 1552.

Roman Catholic missions continued to flourish in the sixteenth and seventeenth centuries, but not all of those who followed in the footsteps of Xavier worked in the same spirit he exemplified. Don Alexis de Menezes, Archbishop of Goa, occupied himself with the ecclesiastical subjugation of the Syrian Church, which was accomplished in 1599. Robert de Nobilibus and his associates, at the beginning of the seventeenth century, attempted to convert the Brahmans by calling themselves Western Brahmans, wearing saffron robes and sandalwood marks on their foreheads, performing child-marriages, encouraging Hindu burial rites, and accepting caste divisions. With the waning of Portuguese power, Roman Catholic missions were in decline at the close of the eighteenth century, then grew again in the nineteenth century with the return of the revived Jesuit society and the coming of other orders too. In 1941 there were, according to the census, 4,317,067 Roman Catholic Christians in India as compared with 4,572,339 non-Roman Christians.

The event in Roman Catholicism which attracted most interest in 1952 was the exposition, on the four hundredth anniversary of his death, of the body of Francis Xavier. Although he died on the borders of China, Xavier's body was brought back to Goa for its last resting place. The recent exposition was conducted by Cardinal Manuel Gonsalves Cerejeira of Lisbon as Papal Legate, Archbishop D. Joseda Costa Nunes, Patriarch of Goa, and fifty Bishops from India, Pakistan, and Ceylon, with the participation of hundreds of priests and monks, and the attendance of more than 50,000 pilgrims. The coffin of the saint, who was canonized in 1622, was carried in impressive procession to the Cathedral in Old Goa, the body was removed and placed in a glass-paneled silver sarcophagus, and the feet were exposed so the pilgrims could file past to kiss them. Although the body is remarkably well-preserved after four hundred years, the right arm was removed some time ago to be sent to the Pope, and one toe is missing, having been bitten off by an ardent devotee on an earlier occasion. At the close of this exposition the body was returned to the Basilica of Bom Jesus, where the sarcophagus will remain permanently sealed and the body henceforward will be shown only through the glass walls on special occasions but no longer will be directly touched.

At the same time that this spectacular event was taking place, other representatives of the Roman church were working in ways which were less publicized but may be thought to be in more accord with the spirit of Xavier himself. At Kurseong, 5,000 feet up in the foothills of the Himalayas, I talked with young men from the United States who were priests studying in the Jesuit Training College at that place. Along with many Europeans and Indians, they lived in unheated buildings in the bitter cold of the winter as they prepared for their service at various stations in India. Their course of study

is so long that one said to me that he would be an old man before he was through. In Calcutta, out on Kalighat Road, Mother Teresa and other sisters of the Missionaries of Charity opened the Nirmal Hridaya or Pure Soul Home as a place of refuge for destitutes with incurable diseases who cannot be admitted to hospitals. At the beginning of 1953, nearly forty such destitutes were being cared for. Wrapped in tattered clothes, some in old curtains, they were a most pitiful sight. Most were dying, some had a few weeks, others only a few days to live. One died in the night and the body lay there waiting to be taken to the burning ghat. Not all were old. One was a young boy in the last stages of tuberculosis. Another, a malnutrition case, died while being fed his first meal. An Anglo-Indian woman who contributed several hours' work each day, said: "We try to make their last hours as pleasant as possible. We try to grant them their last wish. Some want a little *Sandesh* [sweets]. I wish we could always give them what they want."

The missionary enterprise of Protestant Christianity in India began in the year 1706. During the preceding century the Danes acquired a small trading settlement at Tarangambadi (Tranquebar), "the village of the lapping wavelets," south of Madras. In 1706 two young Germans, Heinrich Plütschau and Bartholomäus Ziegenbalg, came to Tranquebar, having been sent out from Copenhagen by the devout Danish king, Frederick IV. In his instructions to Ziegenbalg, the king said: "Having by the grace of God safely arrived in the country he shall, in the name of Jesus, heartily calling upon the same, at once begin the work for which he is sent out; and shall labor among the pagans as existing circumstances shall make it practicable. He shall always specially betake himself to God's word not doubting that God will make the power laid therein to prove effectual among the heathens. He has to instruct the ignorant in the first principles of the Christian doctrine with all possible simplicity so that the needful foundation may be laid the earlier. In order that the poor blind heathens may understand that the missionary himself has in his heart what he teaches, he must always show himself a pattern of good works, so that also by this his conduct they may be won over. He shall not forget daily to pray for the cooperating grace of God." Among those who soon followed the two pioneers, the most eminent was Christian Frederic Schwartz, and by the time of his death in 1789 the Danish mission counted about twenty thousand converts.

At the end of the eighteenth century and in the nineteenth, Protestant churches in England, Scotland, the United States of America, and other countries joined in the missionary undertaking in India. The first missionary from England was the famous William Carey. He was the son of a village schoolmaster and himself a shoemaker. When he published *An Enquiry into the Obligations of Christians to Use Means for the Conversion of the Heathen,* and preached a sermon on Isaiah 54:2-3, ending with the twofold exhortation, "Attempt great things for God; expect great things from God," the formation of the Baptist Missionary Society of the Baptist Church in England was inspired. With a surgeon named John Thomas as his companion, Carey landed at Calcutta in 1793, was prevented from establishing a mission there by the opposition of the East India Company, and went later to Serampore, a Danish settlement fifteen miles away. At Serampore, Carey and Thomas worked with William Ward, Joshua Marshman, and others. This group undertook a variety of activities. Their first convert was made in 1800 as a result of treatment by Thomas, who was thus the first medical missionary in India. Translations of the Bible were prepared and printed, Carey in particular showing himself a great linguist. The New Testament was published in Bengali in 1801 and, in part or in whole, in no less than thirty-five different Indian languages within thirty years. In 1818 a charter was obtained from the King of Denmark and Serampore College was established. Today this institution enjoys the status of a University and as such has responsibility for the direction of higher theological education throughout India, seventeen colleges being affiliated with it.

Among other English missionaries were Henry Martyn and Reginald Heber. Martyn was an Evangelical clergyman who came to India as a chaplain of the East India Company. Upon arrival in 1806 he wrote in his diary the famous words: "I have hitherto lived to little purpose, like a clod upon the earth. Now let me burn out for God." First in Calcutta, then at Dinapore, west of Patna, and at Cawnpore, he devoted himself with such fervor to evangelistic preaching and with such assiduousness to the work of translation of the New Testament that his health was destroyed and he died at the age of thirty-one on a journey to England by way of Persia.

By a change in the charter of the East India Company in 1813, provision was made for the establishment in their territory of the episcopate of the Church of England, and Reginald Heber was the second to occupy the position of Bishop of Calcutta. He had already written "Holy, Holy, Holy," and "From Greenland's Icy Mountains," and although he died suddenly in 1826 after less than three years in India he made a strong missionary contribution.

Of the missionaries who came from Scotland, special prominence attaches to the name of Alexander Duff. Arriving after two shipwrecks in Calcutta in 1830, he devoted himself to the work of education. It was his belief that a Christian mission college should exemplify the highest standards of education, employ the English language as its medium, introduce Indian youth to Western philosophy and science, and thus ultimately enable Christianity to penetrate the whole of Hindu society. In his first year in Calcutta Duff started

184

the Scottish Church College which today offers instruction to 1,800 students of whom only eighty are Christians.

Churches in the United States of America which sent missions to India included the Methodist, Baptist, Disciples of Christ, and many others. James Mills Thoburn came to India in 1859 for the American Methodists, became the minister of a congregation in Calcutta, and was later elected the first Missionary Bishop for India and Malaysia. In 1870 his sister, Isabella Thoburn, also came to India and although at that time education for Indian girls was unheard of and social reforms for women not yet begun, she courageously opened a school for girls at Lucknow. Beginning with six small girls as pupils, this school grew into what is today Isabella Thoburn College, an institution with a fine campus and 370 students from fifteen Indian states and three foreign countries, speaking sixteen mother tongues, and representing five religions. From among its graduates have come the first Indian woman college professor, the first Muslim woman doctor, the first woman member of the Legislative Council, and the first professionally trained teachers.

The American Baptist Foreign Missionary Society sent John E. Clough to India in 1865. He worked among an extremely depressed group of people, the outcaste Madigas, and found them very responsive to the Christian message which for the first time brought hope and help to their wretched lives. Hundreds of them were baptized in a baptistery built on the site of a former pagan shrine, and there developed a mass movement to Christianity which brought twenty thousand members into the Baptist Church in that area in twenty years.

In 1882 the Disciples of Christ sent eight missionaries to India, Mr. and Mrs. Albert Norton, Mr. and Mrs. G. L. Wharton, Miss Mary Graybiel, Miss Ada Boyd, Miss Mary Kingsbury, and Miss Laura Kinsey. They opened a new field of work in the Central Provinces, where the Disciples of Christ now have schools, hospitals, presses, and churches at Bilaspur, Damoh, Jubbulpore, Takhatpur, Pendra Road, and other places.

The Young Men's Christian Association and the Young Women's Christian Association, too, entered India in the nineteenth century. The first Y. W. C. A. was organized in Bombay in 1875, and the

185

first secretary to give full time to the work in India came to Calcutta in 1893 from the British Y. W. C. A. The first Y. M. C. A. secretary came to Madras in 1890 from the United States of America.

Likewise the Salvation Army began work in India in 1882. The Army now has 4,000 officers there, all Indians except for 125 Westerners. Their hostel in Calcutta offers a place to a needy man for two rupees, about forty cents, per month.

The total picture of the growth of Christianity in India is impressive. When we examine the comparable census figures from 1881 to 1941, we find that in 1881 there were 1,778,000 Christians in India or 0.71 per cent of the population; in 1941 the number was 7,427,000 or 1.91 per cent of the total. For each of the ten-year census periods the percentage of Christians in the total population was as shown in this table:

1881	1891	1901	1911	1921	1931	1941
0.71	0.77	0.98	1.21	1.47	1.77	1.91

This means that between 1881 and 1941 Christianity more than quadrupled its adherents and more than doubled its proportion of the total population. During this time it was the fastest-growing religion in India, its nearest competitors being Sikhism and Islam, while in the same period Hinduism declined from 75 per cent of the population in 1881 to 69.46 per cent in 1941. Of the total number of Christians in 1921, 8.1 per cent belonged to the Orthodox and Reformed Syrian Churches, 48.4 per cent to the Roman Catholic Church including the Romo-Syrians, and 41.7 per cent to the several Protestant denominations. According to the 1951 census there were over 8,200,000 Christians in India, 2.3 per cent of the population.

Most of the Protestant groups united their forces in the National Christian Council which was organized in 1914 as a result of the First World Missionary Conference at Edinburgh in 1910. The National Christian Council is intended to stimulate thinking on missionary and church matters, to maintain communication with the International Missionary Council and the World Council of Churches, and to help form Christian public opinion and bring it to bear on the moral and social problems of the day. In the *Directory of Churches and Missions in India and Pakistan* published by the National Christian Council is a comprehensive summary of the current status of the Protestant Christian enterprise. In the 1951 edition of this *Directory* no less than eighty pages are required to list the Christian institutions which exist. These are economic establishments like agricultural settlements, cooperative societies, and printing presses; educational institutions including colleges, high schools, industrial schools, and teachers' training institutions; evangelistic organizations such as pastoral and evangelistic workers' training institutions; general foundations such as missionary homes of rest; medical institutions including hospitals, dispensaries, leprosy institutes, and tuberculosis sanatoria; philanthropic foundations such as homes for the blind and the deaf, homes for women, homes for converts, orphanages, and social and welfare organizations; and, finally, periodicals. Although in many of these fields there are now also excellent institutions or programs sponsored by the government or other agencies, still it is true that in most of them, particularly in agriculture, education, and medicine, Christian missions pioneered the way. It is also notable that in 1931 Christians were more than four times as literate as Muslims, three times as literate as Hindus; and literacy among Christian women is more than ten times the average among non-Christian women. In South India the proportion of Christians convicted of crime is said to be less than one fifth that of Hindus and less than one third that of Muslims. Indian Christians like Sadhu Sundar Singh, the wealthy Sikh who combined the Indian ideal of the holy man with his Christian faith, and V. S. Azariah, the outcaste Tamil who became the first Indian bishop, not to mention leaders now in the prime of their activity, have become known to the whole world church.

Indian Christians have also led the way with constructive experiments toward the reunion of the divided bodies of Christendom. After twenty-eight years of discussion and negotiation, the Church of South India came into being in 1947 as a union of the Anglican Church, the Methodist Church, and the South India United Church which already combined Presbyterian and Congregational bodies. The integration of four such diverse traditions and above all of both episcopal and nonepiscopal churches in such a union is a remarkable

achievement. The total membership is said to be now over one million. In North India also a Plan of Church Union is under consideration and the United Church of Northern India (Presbyterian and Congregational), the Church of India, Burma, Pakistan and Ceylon (Anglican), the Methodist Church in Southern Asia, the Methodist Church (British and Australian Conferences), and the Baptist Church (British Baptist Missionary Society) are participating in the discussions and negotiations.

Although the Christian mission and the Christian church have thus made epic accomplishments in India, Indian Christianity now faces an ordeal. It experiences the difficulty of smallness. Although it has made a phenomenal growth, Christianity still represents only little more than 2 per cent of the population of India. Since about half of all the Christians are Roman Catholics, the Protestant Christians are only about 1 per cent of the population. About 60 per cent of the Christians are in South India, moreover, which means that in other parts of the land the percentages are even smaller. It is possible therefore for a casual visitor to pass through large areas of the great cities and vast stretches of the country without seeing

188

anything to cause him to suspect that Christianity even exists here. There is a warmth of fellowship when Christian groups come together, yet when they go out from the meeting the individual members are almost swallowed up in the surrounding sea of paganism.

Christianity in India confronts the charge of foreignness. It was introduced to India, it is pointed out, by outsiders. It is said that it came along with traders and soldiers intent upon building empire. It has been administered by foreigners. While there is some truth in such statements as these, there is also some omission and misrepresentation of facts. Christianity is not the only religion which was brought to India from the outside. Both Zoroastrianism and Islam came from abroad. Actually, Christianity in the form of the Syrian church came to India much earlier than either of these two religions. Furthermore, in modern times Christianity did not come to India as the handmaid of imperialism but made its initial way here in spite of the strong opposition of the East India Company and the British Government. The commercial and political interests did not want to risk having anything done which might disturb the populace and endanger trade or administration. Lucrative revenue was being derived from the Indian temples which had come under government supervision, and it was not desired to lose this source of income. Government laws of various sorts discriminated against Indians who did accept Christianity. One historian writes: "For a very long time the Government not only encouraged the perpetuation of Hinduism in all its aspects, but also placed every obstacle in the way of the progress of Christianity, especially by refusing to give the new convert to the faith a fair deal, subjecting him to all kinds of uncalled-for handicaps." In fact, it was not until 1850 that Christians became free from legal discriminations and not until 1862 that the last Hindu temple was returned to Hindu administration. When it is claimed that the Christian movement in India has been dominated by foreigners, it may be forgotten that for years now a process of transfer of leadership to Indian Christians has been under way. Nevertheless it is probably true, as trusted Indian Christian leaders have said to me, that Western church officials were too slow in doing this. Since much of the transfer has been made only in these years after independence, it has the appearance of something which was forced by outside events rather than having been done voluntarily. Much would have been gained if the church in India could have entered the era of independence as itself a truly Indian body. It must also be admitted, that as far as its tangible form is concerned, Christianity in India still looks Western. Many church buildings could have been brought here bodily from somewhere in Europe or America; most of the songs that are sung are from the West. An Indian Christian writer says flatly: "So far, we have not created a Christian Indian theology, a Christian Indian art, a Christian Indian music, and a Christian Indian architecture; we have not produced distinctively Indian Christian devotional and theological literature."

The church in India confronts the test of independence. However slowly, the administration of its own affairs is now coming into its own hands. Missionaries remain and are needed, but leadership is passing to the Indian Christians themselves and all who come from the outside must be willing to be colleagues and not directors. The day of the "foreign" mission is giving way to that of the indig-

190

enous church as it was always desired that it should. But this means that a very heavy responsibility now devolves upon the Indian church. In national life it was easy to blame the British for everything during the days of the independence movement; now it is proving extremely difficult for Indian leaders themselves to find solutions to India's stupendous problems. As in the attainment of national independence, so too in the life of the newly independent church, high hopes properly arise and are necessarily succeeded by a sense of heavy responsibility. Discussing the problems of church union in North India in the November, 1952, issue of *The Indian Journal of Theology*, a missionary suggests that many of the difficulties "will just fade out" if and when the connection of the Indian church with the Western churches becomes "attenuated," and this opinion would doubtless be shared by a great many Indian Christians. Much as it is to be hoped that this will be the case, it cannot be supposed that all obstacles will automatically disappear; more than likely unexpected new ones will also emerge; and so the meeting of the new problems by the Indian church on its own will be a part of the test it endures.

The Indian church faces the difficult situation of poverty. It is part of the greatness of the Christian accomplishment in India that the gospel has been preached to the poor and that the church is predominantly made up of persons from the depressed classes. This means that most of the church members have extremely meager resources, and so the attempt of the church to stand increasingly on its own feet is a hard test. Furthermore, the people of the depressed classes have so long been oppressed and denied their rights that it is not easy for them immediately to assume the leadership and exercise the initiative to which they are called in the new day.

The Christian church in India is confronted by the threat of Communism. As shown earlier in this book, the Communist movement has already attained ominous proportions in India and the danger is not to be discounted that in the future it will actually triumph. In such an eventuality, to judge from what has happened in other countries, the ordeal which would ensue for the Christian church would presumably be of the most drastic sort.

191

In the immediate present, perhaps the most critical problem of all those facing the Christian church in India arises from the fact that it exists in an environment permeated with the philosophical assumptions of Hinduism, and vibrant with the feelings of the new nationalism. It is fundamental to Hinduism to hold that ultimate reality is beyond human comprehension, that any belief about it is at best only partially true, and that therefore any one belief is as good as any other if it is useful to the person who holds it. When Dr. S. Radhakrishnan, distinguished Hindu philosopher and vice-president of India, met with the Central Committee of the World Council of Churches at Lucknow at the beginning of January, 1953, he expressed this point of view very eloquently. Holding that the realization of God by the human soul has taken place in different ways among different peoples, he was unable to agree with what he understood to be the Christian position that a unique and unrepeatable disclosure of the divine had taken place through Jesus Christ. The very fact that the premise of this argument is accepted by many liberal Christian thinkers makes it more difficult to deny the logicality of the conclusion Radhakrishnan drew; yet the acceptance of his position and the admission that there is no real difference among religions is felt by many Christians to remove the incentive to evangelistic work. Another visitor to the same meeting, Sri K. M. Munshi, governor of Uttar Pradesh, in which Lucknow is located, stated bluntly his feeling that Christians should not try to convert others in the East. He described the white men who came in the early days to preach the gospel as displaying an aggressive proselytizing zeal and a self-assurance that they were bringing salvation to a benighted people. "Such attitude," said the governor to the delegates, "is a relic of the past and I am sure, when you have finished your tour of the countries of Asia you will realize that in Asia new ambitious nations have risen, that their religions and cultures may improve, modernized by contact with Christianity but cannot be replaced by it."

Later in 1953 it was reported that K. N. Katju, minister of home affairs, had said in parliament that foreign missionaries would be welcome in India to carry on medical, educational, and social work, but that if they intend to convert people to Christianity, they will have to leave the country. A letter was afterward published in *Harijan*, the weekly founded by Mahatma Gandhi, which was understood to come from Dr. Katju and which explained his view further. Addressed to a foreign missionary, it read: "You wrote to me something about missionaries and their visas. You know I owe personally a great deal to my own college, Forman Christian at Lahore (1901-1905), and I realize what wonderful help India has drawn from missionaries abroad. We Indians in our own constitution have guaranteed perfect freedom of conscience and perfect liberty to propagate one's faith. Being myself a devoted reader of both the Old and New Testaments, and realizing the essential unity of all religious thought, I am becoming more and more convinced that the propagation of one's faith in these modern days can best be made not by preaching but by example of a life spent in the service of one's fellow beings. India welcomes the assistance of those who will come to this ancient land to help in a variety of ways, just like yourself, to show us how to improve our standard of living in the field of agriculture, medicine, education and other spheres of human activity. The light of the gospel shines and illuminates through such action rather than by mere evangelistic effort. Conditions in India are rapidly changing. Freedom has brought about strong national consciousness. We have all to adjust ourselves to the new conditions." The editor of *Harijan* commented: "It is our very strong belief and opinion that while everybody in India is at perfect liberty to preach and propagate his or her own religion, we do not need nor welcome anybody from abroad to come here to do evangelical work. Work in fields of social service is another matter, and it is all welcome. Done in a spirit of pure service, it is its own reward." Referring to the opinion just expressed, the correspondent of *The Christian Century*, P. Oomman Philip, wrote from India: "This view is held widely by the large majority of educated Hindus who are leaders in the life and thought of present-day India. The concept of the equality of all religions which inspires such a view is not, however, acceptable to Christian leaders in India."[1]

---

[1] *The Christian Century*, LXX, 43, October 28, 1953, pp. 1236-1237; LXX, 48, December 2, 1953, pp. 1380-1381; LXX, 52, December 30, 1953, p. 1515.

In November, 1953, Rajkumari (Princess) Amrit Kaur, the Government health minister and the only Christian in the cabinet, said in a public address: "The only thing that the Government of India desires is that foreign missionaries keep themselves entirely aloof from political propaganda and carry out only social welfare and religious work." In June, 1954, a letter by Mr. Nehru was made public in which the prime minister stated: "There has been no difference at all in our policy of full religious tolerance. The question of missionaries coming from abroad came before us first in its political, not religious, aspects. . . . Another aspect of the question . . . was the tendency of some missionaries from abroad to run down India and Indian culture. . . . Humanitarian and educational work is always welcome, and though we may not be enthusiastic about purely evangelical work, we do not wish to come in its way."[1]

The Central Committee of the World Council of Churches, which met at Lucknow, India, in December, 1952—January, 1953, dealt with the whole problem of Christian work in Asia and pointed to the way to go forward in the following statement: "The missionary task of the church is more important than ever in Asia today. Amid elemental hunger, the uprooting of life and the struggle to rebuild, the fundamental need is still man's need for God. It must be known that within the events of our time His Presence is to be discerned in judgment and blessing. Christ alone makes this knowledge possible in all its redemptive power. To preach Him and bear witness to Him amidst the claims of other faiths is a task of burning urgency. . . . The overwhelming evangelistic task in Asia is the concern of the whole church. This responsibility now falls primarily upon the churches in Asia. But the Western churches need to redouble, and not slacken, their missionary endeavor in Asia. Yet this contribution from the West must be undertaken in a spirit of partnership with the younger churches, and along lines which will strengthen them for their own missionary obedience."

[1]*The Christian-Evangelist*, Vol. 91, No. 49, December 9, 1953, p. 1188; *The Christian Century*, LXXI, 25, June 23, 1954, p. 773.

Appendix

COMMENTS

by V. E. Devadutt, Th. D.[1]

Professor of the History of Religion
Ohio Wesleyan University

Contemporary India is a big question mark to many people in the United States and while I have no doubt that to a discerning reader the essay of Dr. Finegan will be a great help, I may be permitted to make a few observations on the subject. India's neutrality in the contest of East-West struggle to which Dr. Finegan makes reference, is a source of anxiety to many Americans who wish well by India. Perhaps there is no other area in Indo-American relations which is so much a source of misunderstanding between the two countries. It can be stated with confidence that all informed and patriotic opinion in India whether within the Hindu or Christian or other communities is solidly behind the Indian Government's policy of neutrality. "Neutrality" or "neutralism" is, however, an inept word to describe the purposes of India's policy. For instance, neither the present government nor an overwhelming majority of people in India is neutral when it comes to a choice for the country between a democratic way of life and a totalitarian way of life. India has cast its vote solidly in favor of democracy. Among others, there are two important tests of whether a government and a people are truly alive to democratic implications. One of them is their steadfast adherence to the principle of freedom of thought. As an educator I personally value this principle immensely, and in Independent India there was no sign at any time that either the government or pressure groups of one kind or the other intended to put shackles on one's thoughts. The other test is the right of an accused,

---

[1]Formerly Chairman of the Department of Philosophy and the Dean of Theology, Serampore College, Serampore, India, and past president of the Baptist Union of India, Pakistan, Burma, and Ceylon.

even if he is accused by the government, to be considered innocent till he is proved guilty by an impartial and independent judicial tribunal following a recognized judicial process of trial. Independent India has so far not failed of this test. The principles involved in these tests are some of the spiritual intangibles that support and sustain a democracy, and manifest its inherent good. It does not mean that democracy in India is flawless! Democracy is always a present reality and a school toward an ideal.

What then is India's neutrality? India's neutrality can be understood only when we recognize that there is a revolution in India and Asia. There are two fundamental urges to human nature and they are at the basis of this revolution. These two urges are to find individuality and community. Large masses of people in Asian lands have been treated for ages by their own people as very much less than human beings. They are not individuals but impersonal units in an impersonal mass. They knew few civil liberties; their one liberty was to serve others for wages that gave them less than one inadequate meal every twenty-four hours. This was the lot of untouchables for long in India. But Asian peasant and farmer fared hardly better. The land that he tilled was often not his and a great part of the fruit of his labor was often taken away by the landowner, the middleman and the money lender. An Asian farmer is born into debt, lives in debt, dies in debt and leaves debt as the only legacy to his posterity. People now are refusing to be treated in this manner. They desire to be treated not as impersonal units in an impersonal mass but as individuals and human beings.

But an individual without community or society is an abstraction. Individuality in itself is merely a principle of division. Each individual is a person and as a person he has the roots of his being in society. His personality has been moulded by influences coming from home, school, temple or the church. Hence, there is a deep longing in man for community. This urge for community on one level showed itself in movements for national independence in former colonies and is showing itself thus in areas which are still under alien rule. A nation that is subject to another nation is not allowed to have or has no will of its own. The decisions that are made concerning its destinies are made not by the common consent of the people, not by the people as a common body, not as a community, but by a power alien to them. Some community develops only when a people engage themselves in common purpose and action. But even where people have achieved independence the search for community is still going on. Industry, though in some respects is still in initial stages, is changing, in many regions in Asia, old patters of communal organization. For instance, hand-loom industry was one of the most widely spread cottage industries in Indian villages for centuries and was the basis of communal organizations for certain sections of rural communities. Large textile mills of modern days have nearly killed this cottage industry, displacing millions of people economically and breaking the old system of community organization for them. The disintegration of the old social fabric, though still a slow process, is a steady process and is creating new problems and new aspirations.

196

Because there is a revolution going on in Asia, India desires policies that would aid this revolution in constructive ways and meet its fundamental impulses. The Commonwealth or what is popularly called the Colombo Plan is one of these; her own Five Year Plan of which Dr. Finegan gives an excellent summary is another, and still another is Point-Four Programme of the U. S. A. If this revolution is to be constructively channelled and not betrayed into the hands of reactionaries of the extreme right or the extreme left, there must be peace in the world, much more in Asia. War would betray this revolution into the hands of extremists, according to Indian opinion. For this reason India wants the whole area in East Asia kept out of cold war, for the fear is that cold war may develop into a shooting war any time. Democracy will have no chance in Asia if Asia is involved in a general war. The result will be either communism or renewed colonialism. Furthermore, asks India, will anything be left for humanity if there should be a war now? South East Asia should remain a third area according to informed Indian opinion not only for the sake of India's and Asia's own interests but that it may act as a restraining force in the two Great Power Blocs. No one can be presumed to want war under modern conditions of warfare despite all the harsh language and threats used but one may get into war despite one's wishes to the contrary. Sometimes our strength is our very weakness. It is the conviction of many Indians that it is in the interests of democracies that there should be a third area.

It should be understood that by its very definition neutrality implies a strong desire to remain independent. It is a refusal to be hustled into a position by others or to be dominated by others. If this strong desire to be independent is threatened by external aggression, India, I have no doubt, will not meekly yield. It is the conviction of Indians generally that coupled with the desire to maintain a democratic way of life this neutrality is a source of strength to democracies.

I have not written this to offer an apology for India. A real understanding of contemporary India, however, demands a real understanding of her neutralist policy. I hope what I have stated will add slightly to the excellent essay of Dr. Finegan. Indians feel hurt when it is laid down as an axiom lightly that if a people "are not with us, they must be against us." India desires ardently to be understood. America and India are devoted to democracy. American help to India in recent years has been enormous. Given the good will toward one another and patience with each other they can be a force for peace in the world. The ardent wishes and prayers of men of good will everywhere are directed toward the achievement of understanding between these two countries. I am sure Dr. Finegan's book will help toward this end.

Some Recent Books and Articles about India

Books

Archaeology in India (Bureau of Education, India, Publication No. 66). Calcutta: Government of India Press, 1950.

Prabodh Chandra Bagchi, *India and China, A Thousand Years of Cultural Relations.* Bombay: H. Kitabs, 2d ed. 1950.

Chester Bowles, *Ambassador's Report.* New York: Harper & Brothers, 1954.

Charles S. Braden, *War, Communism and World Religions.* New York: Harper & Brothers, 1953, pp.124-186.

W. Norman Brown, ed., *India, Pakistan, Ceylon.* Ithaca: Cornell University Press, 1950.

W. Norman Brown, *The United States and India and Pakistan.* Cambridge: Harvard University Press, 1953.

Atul Chandra Chatterjee, *The New India.* London: George Allen and Unwin Ltd., 1948.

Norman Cousins, *Talks with Nehru.* New York: The John Day Company, Inc., 1951.

John Cumming, ed., *Revealing India's Past.* London: The India Society, 1939.

Kingsley Davis, *The Population of India.* Princeton: Princeton University Press, 1951.

Directory of Churches and Missions in India and Pakistan 1951. Published for the National Christian Council by the World Dominion Press, Farley, Ootacamund.

B. B. Ghosh, *Indian Economics and Pakistani Economics.* Calcutta: A. Mukherjee and Company Ltd., 1949.

George E. Jones, *Tumult in India.* New York: Dodd, Mead and Company, 1948.

D. G. Karve, *Poverty and Population in India.* London: Oxford University Press, 1936.

Werner Levi, *Free India in Asia.* Minneapolis: University of Minnesota Press, 1952.

Jean Lyon, *Just Half a World Away.* New York: The Thomas Y. Crowell Co., 1954.

Monica Martin, *Out in the Mid-day Sun.* Boston: Little, Brown and Company, 1951.

Asoka Mehta, *The Political Mind of India.* Bombay: A Socialist Party Publication, 1952.

Sohan Raj Mohnot, *Indian Economic Policy.* Allahabad: Friends' Book Depot, 1952.

Frank Moraes, ed., *The Indian and Pakistan Year Book and Who's Who 1952-1953.* Vol. XXXVIII. Published by The Times of India, Bombay, Delhi, and Calcutta.

F. R. Moraes and Robert Stimson, *Introduction to India.* New York and London: Oxford University Press, 1943.

Kenneth W. Morgan, ed., *The Religion of the Hindus.* New York: The Ronald Press Company, 1953.

John F. Muehl, *Interview with India.* New York: The John Day Company, Inc., 1950.

Manilal B. Nanavati and C. N. Vakil, eds., "India Speaking," in *The Annals of The American Academy of Political and Social Science,* Vol. 233, May 1944.

Jawaharlal Nehru, *The Discovery of India.* New York: The John Day Company, Inc., 1946.

Jawaharlal Nehru, *Glimpses of World History.* New York: The John Day Company, Inc., 1942.

Jawaharlal Nehru, *Independence and After.* New York: The John Day Company, Inc., 1950.

Jawaharlal Nehru, *Toward Freedom.* New York: The John Day Company, Inc., 1942.

Jawaharlal Nehru, *Visit to America.* New York: The John Day Company, Inc., 1950.

T. A. Raman, *Let's Read About India.* Grand Rapids: The Fideler Company, 1950.

Poola Tirupati Raju, *India's Culture and Her Problems.* Jaipur: University of Rajputana, 1952.

Eleanor Roosevelt, *India and the Awakening East.* New York: Harper and Brothers, 1953.

Lawrence K. Rosinger, *India and the United States, Political and Economic Relations.* New York: The Macmillan Company, 1950.

Lawrence K. Rosinger, *Restless India.* New York: Henry Holt and Company, 1946.

Vincent Sheean, *Lead, Kindly Light.* New York: Random House, Inc., 1949.

Wilfred C. Smith, *Modern Islām in India.* London: Victor Gollancz Ltd., 1946.

Percival Spear, *India, Pakistan, and the West.* London: Oxford University Press, 1949.

Cornelia Spencer, *Nehru of India.* New York: The John Day Company, 1948.

Murray T. Titus, *Indian Islam.* London: Oxford University Press, 1930.

Murray T. Titus, *The Young Moslem Looks at Life.* New York: Friendship Press, 1937.

T. W. Walbank, *India: A Survey of the Heritage and Growth of Indian Nationalism.* New York: Henry Holt and Company, Inc., 1948.

T. W. Walbank, *India in the New Era.* Chicago: Scott, Foresman and Company, 1951.

Clare and Harris Wofford, Jr., *India Afire.* New York: The John Day Company, Inc., 1951.

Articles

C. H. Alexandrowicz, "India and the Tibetan Tragedy," in *Foreign Affairs,* XXXI, 3, April 1953, pp.495-500.

Philip H. Ashby, "Christianity in the New India," in *The Christian Century,* XXI, 30, July 28, 1954, pp.898-900.

John A. Banningan, "The Hindu Code Bill," in *Far Eastern Survey,* XXI, 17, December 3, 1952, pp.173-176.

Chester Bowles, "New India," in *Foreign Affairs,* XXXI, 1, October 1952, pp. 79-94.

Harvey Breit, ed., "Perspective of India, An *Atlantic* Supplement," in *The Atlantic,* Vol. 192, No. 4, October 1953, pp.103-172.

Jerome B. Cohen, "Economic Development in India," in *Political Science Quarterly,* LXVIII, 3, September 1953, pp.376-395.

M. L. Dantwala, "Agricultural Credit in India—the Missing Link," in *Pacific Affairs,* XXV, 4, December 1952, pp. 349-359.

Vera Micheles Dean, "The United States and India," in *Far Eastern Survey,* XXI, 5, April 2, 1952, pp.41-46.

Vera Micheles Dean, "India and the Korean Truce," in *Foreign Policy Bulletin,* XXXII, 24, September 1, 1953, pp.1-2.

Vera Micheles Dean, "Stocktaking in India," in *Foreign Policy Bulletin,* XXXIII, 1, September 15, 1953, pp.1-2, 8.

Vera Micheles Dean, "Will India Go Communist?" in *Foreign Policy Bulletin,* XXXIII, 2, October 1, 1953, pp.4-8.

Vert Micheles Dean, "What U. S. and India Agree On," in *The Christian Century,* LXXI, 27, July 7, 1954, pp. 818-819.

Donald F. Ebright, "Christianity in India Under Fire," in *The Christian Century,* LXXI, 24, June 16, 1954, pp.729-730.

Clarence Falk, "Only India Can Save South Asia," in *The Christian Century,* LXII, 2, January 12, 1955.

Ruth Fischer, "The Indian Communist Party," in *Far Eastern Survey,* XXII, 7, June 1953, pp.79-84.

Margaret Frakes, "The U. N.'s First Lady," in *The Christian Century,* LXX, 45, November 11, 1953, pp.1295-1297.

Holden Furber, "The Unification of India, 1947-1951," in *Pacific Affairs,* XXIV, 4, December 1951, pp.352-371.

"India Next?" Editorial in *The Christian Century,* LXX, 30, July 29, 1953, pp. 862-863.

Shao Chuan Leng, "India and China" in *Far Eastern Survey,* XXI, 8, May 21, 1952, pp.73-78.

A. D. Mani, "The Indian Press Today," in *Far Eastern Survey,* XXI, 11, July 2, 1952, pp.109-113.

Robert F. Meagher, "India's Five-Year Plan: The Final Draft," in *Far Eastern Survey,* XXII, 4, March 25, 1953, pp.42-43.

P. S. Narasimhan, "Labor Reforms in Contemporary India," in *Pacific Affairs,* XXVI, 1, March 1953, pp.44-58.

"New State in Red Shadow," in *Newsweek,* XLII, 15, October 12, 1953, p.45.

Richard L. Park, "India Argues With Kashmir," in *Far Eastern Survey,* XXI, 11, July 2, 1952, pp.113-116.

Richard L. Park, "Indian Democracy and the General Election," in *Pacific Affairs,* XXV, 2, June 1952, pp.130-139.

Richard L. Park, "Indian Election Results," in *Far Eastern Survey,* XXI, 7, May 7, 1952, pp.61-70.

Richard L. Park, "India's General Elections," in *Far Eastern Survey,* XXI, 1, January 9, 1952, pp.1-8.

P. Oomman Philip, "India: The Christian Outlook," in *The Christian Century,* LXX, 46, November 18, 1953, pp.1319-1320.

Clarence E. Pike, "Land Reform in India," in *Foreign Agriculture,* XVII, 6, June 1953, pp.116-117.

Earle K. Rambo, "Farm Machinery in India," in *Foreign Agriculture,* XVII, 1, January 1953, pp.9-12.

V. K. R. V. Rao, "India's First Five-Year Plan—A Descriptive Analysis," in *Pacific Affairs,* XXV, 1, March 1952, pp.3-23.

Santha Rama Rau, "India," in *Holiday,* XIV, 4, October 1953, pp.34-56, 82-83, 85-86.

H. W. Singer, "India's Five-Year Plan: A Modest Proposal," in *Far Eastern Survey,* XXI, 10, June 18, 1952, pp. 97-101.

N. V. Sovani, "The Food Situation in India," in *Far Eastern Survey,* XXII, 8, July 1953, pp.101-103.

Carl E. Taylor, "Will India Accept Birth Control?" in *The Atlantic,* Vol. 190, No. 3, September 1952, pp.51-53.

Index of Photographs

General Index

205

MAP OF
INDIA

Drawn by
Jack Finegan

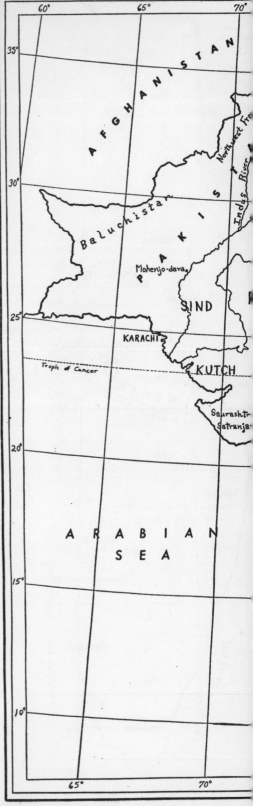

Scale of miles

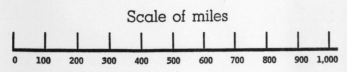

0   100   200   300   400   500   600   700   800   900   1,000

8588